A MUST READ FOR EVERYONE! The author Michelle Shelfer amazed me with her words of clarity, value, and love for humanity. This book will transform your thinking about ~~~~~~ lf, and how disappointments can be ~~~~~~~~~~~~~ in life. It's "Time2Heal," as I would ~~~~~~~~~~~~ u Michelle, for explaining the steps t ~~~~~~~~~~~~~ reparing an eternal, beautiful room ir ~~~~~~~~~~~~

TRISH STEELE
Founder, Safe Passage/Time2Heal

THIS BOOK ON HELPING THOSE who have had or been associated with an abortion is easy to read and would make a wonderful basis for a Bible study on forgiveness for individuals or groups.

BEV CIELNICKY
President, Crusade for Life

AS A WOMAN WHO HAS PERSONALLY EXPERIENCED ABORTION, it was a joy to have tea with this author while preparing the rooms. This book not only offers the hope of healing for those suffering the guilt and shame of abortion, but it also addresses relationships and other important issues. Most importantly, it points to the "greatest love," which is the love of Jesus by His sacrifice on the cross for our sins!

I recommend this book to counselors helping the post-abortive or to individuals seeking healing from abortion, and also to those wanting a better understanding of the effects of abortion.

MARY ANN AMBROSELLI
25-year Executive Director, Ventura County Pregnancy Center
23-year Counselor/Leader, Healing Hearts Ministries

READY FOR REALITY? It doesn't get more real than the journey you are about to take with Michelle Shelfer in *Prepare a Room*. Having personally experienced the pain in abortion, she courageously shares the path to "greatest love." Now a mother and grandmother, she will gently lead you through the reconstruction of your life by preparing the "new rooms" you will need for this life-transforming reality. If at some point in this journey you feel that you can't go forward, go to her personal story at the end of this book and find new reasons to continue on. New life is awaiting you as you follow the path that Michelle has so carefully prepared for you!

GAYLORD ENNS
Author of *Love Revolution: Rediscovering the Lost Command of Jesus*

AT OUR PRENATAL CLINIC, we often see women who face past abortions and miscarriages, or who have even suffered a stillbirth. Sometimes our patients are considering abortion because their current situation isn't a healthy one in which to raise a child. No two women's stories are the same. Having this book will give us a great resource, a book full of hope, a lifeline to offer any woman, and a way to help her see beyond her past decisions with a future hope.

I highly recommend Michelle Shelfer's very well written, moving book for anyone working with post-abortive people.

And I will give you a new heart, and a new spirit I will put within you. And I will remove the heart of stone from your flesh and give you a heart of flesh. (Ezekiel 36:26)

ROBIN STROM
Executive Director, Marin Pregnancy Clinic

FINALLY! I have many counseling opportunities to care for couples and individuals who have suffered with the guilt and shame of abortion. Though I share the love, mercy, and forgiveness of God in our Messiah, still there was always a need for a testimony of love, warm acceptance, practical advice, and the Good News for hurting people, from a woman who walked that trail of tears and came through it as an instrument of God's joy, help, and healing. Michelle Shelfer is that woman, and this book is finally the much-needed resource for those in my situation who want desperately to help those who are hurting the most.

Thank you, Michelle, for helping to address this great need in our society with compassion, kindness, and clarity, as you wonderfully "speak the truth in love" to all who are willing to take the time to open their hearts to Yeshua's amazing love and grace!

DR. SAM NADLER
Author; President, Word of Messiah Ministries
Congregation leader, Hope of Israel Congregation, Charlotte, NC

THIS IS A BOOK THAT WILL TOUCH MANY LIVES! With compassionate candor, Michelle Shelfer explores eternal realities and temporal trials in a way that will open the reader's heart to a "big-picture" view of life on earth. She draws on historical precedents, cultural nuances, and personal testimony in a heartfelt, easy-to-read style. This is a tremendous resource to anyone dealing with grief and loss and who is looking for true love.

T. MYLES WEISS, MA MFT

This book belongs to:

Prepare a Room

a path to peace and healing
for those hurt by abortion

Michelle Shelfer

The Gail Grace Nordskog Collection

Nordskog
Publishing inc.

Ventura, California

Prepare a Room:
A Path to Peace and Healing for Those Hurt by Abortion
by Michelle Shelfer
© The Shelfer Family Trust 2020

ISBN: 978-1-946497-95-6
LCCN: 2020943334

Editing, Design, and Typesetting: benediction.biz
Theological Editing: Ronald W. Kirk
Proofreading: Cheryl Geyer

Printed in the United States of America by Versa Press.

Published by

Nordskog Publishing inc.

Nordskog Publishing, Inc.
2716 Sailor Avenue, Ventura, CA 93001
805-642-2070 • 805-276-5129
NordskogPublishing.com

Christian
Indie Publishing
Association

For Melody Chaia, our little Song of Life

Table of Contents

Publishers' Words

"For I know the plans that I have for you," declares the LORD, *"plans for welfare and not for calamity, to give you a future and a hope. Then you will call upon Me and come and pray to Me, and I will listen to you. You will seek Me and find Me when you search for Me with all your heart...." "Call to Me and I will answer you, and I will tell you great and mighty things, which you do not know."* (Jeremiah 29:11–13; 33:3)

My husband Jerry and I are co-publishers of Nordskog Publishing Inc. We established the Gail Grace Nordskog Collection several years ago. I like to refer to the titles under this collection as the softer side of NPI. My original thought was to produce prayer journals as companion pieces for selected books we publish. Susie Hobson's book *Loving God with All Your Heart*[1] was our first book with a prayer journal.

---

1. Susie Hobson, *Loving God with All Your Heart: Keeping the Greatest Commandment in Everyday Life* (Ventura, CA: Nordskog Publishing, 2010).

Over time, we have expanded the Gail Grace Nordskog Collection to include inspirational books, such as *Hearts of Purpose*,[2] which features real-life stories about ten ordinary women whose lives were forever changed when they came face to face with Jesus. Many of these ladies have gone into the mission fields, some have started orphanages and adoption agencies, and others have lived out their faith in the business world and politics. God wants us to live out our faith to the fullest in every area of our lives and in every sphere of culture.

Michelle Shelfer is the managing editor at Nordskog Publishing. She was the editor for *Hearts of Purpose,* Volume 1, *The Call.* I got to know her quite well as she took the stories, pictures, and dreams I had for my book and made them into a beautiful work of art. Michelle shared her personal story with me during that time. She has a powerful testimony of how a little Jewish girl from the city of San Francisco with a "You go, Girl" attitude changed her life forever when she met the love and forgiveness of Yeshua HaMashiach, Jesus the Messiah.

When I first read Michelle's manuscript for *Prepare a Room*, I didn't realize how her message would affect me. Many thoughts ran through my mind, waking up a broken heart. My first thought was for a childhood friend who, in her late teens, had an abortion that I was not aware of until years later. Her father forced her to abort her baby. When we rekindled our friendship in 2012, I sensed a heaviness in her. I knew what had happened in her past, but we never spoke of it—I didn't know how. *Prepare a Room* would have been a priceless treasure to offer her, to help lift her burden of guilt. Unfortunately, she passed away a few years ago, but I believe she is in the arms of our loving Savior, and her child is lovingly in her arms.

My second thought was personal. Jerry and I each had young daughters from previous marriages when we married thirty years

2. Gail Nordskog, *Hearts of Purpose: Real-Life Stories about Ten Ordinary Women Doing Extraordinary Things for the Glory of God* (Ventura, CA: Nordskog Publishing, 2017).

ago. We hoped, planned, prayed, and expected to have children together to make our new, "blended" family complete. In God's providence, He has His divine plan for each of us who surrender to Him, and it is always perfect, even if it's not what we expected. I never conceived that I am aware of, though I often wondered if the heavy periods I sometimes experienced in the early years of our marriage were actually miscarriages.

As I was reading *Prepare a Room*, so many old, familiar, and painful emotions of loss returned to me. I started questioning God again. Why, God? As I walked through the chapters of this book and my own memories of loss, I sensed God wanted me to rejoice and be thankful. He encouraged me to "prepare a room," as He reminded me again that He has done great and mighty things in our family. He led Jerry and me to choose adoption to add to our family, filling our empty rooms here on earth with our four beautiful children born in China.

Whether you have experienced the loss of a child through a miscarriage, a closed womb, or an abortion, there is forgiveness and healing for you. I am excited for you and convinced that everyone who works through the chapters of *Prepare a Room* will find love for their child, peace for their soul, and a personal relationship with Almighty God.

> I prayed often for deliverance from the pain caused by my decision to abort my baby. I suffered the threat of cervical and breast cancer and experienced the pain of empty arms after the baby was gone. And truly, for me, and countless abortive mothers, nothing on earth can fully restore what has been lost; only Jesus can. (Dr. Alveda King)

I am honored to present *Prepare a Room* under the banner of the Gail Grace Nordskog Collection.

GAIL GRACE NORDSKOG
July Fourth, Independence Day, 2020

For there is one God, and one Mediator between God and man, which is the man Christ Jesus, Who gave himself a ransom for all men, to be that testimony in due time. (1 Timothy 2:5–6)

Nothing stirs my heart more than witnessing the ongoing assault on the sanctity of human life that became law in 1973 with the passing of Roe v. Wade and continues to this day. This so-called "law"—badly decided—normalized infanticide and ripped through the fabric of the American family, leaving devastation in its wake. This has weighed heavily on me for many years as one that calls for a bold Christian response. I have long desired for Nordskog Publishing to add to its collection of titles a book that would tackle head on the topic of abortion from a Christian perspective.

That desire has finally been fulfilled in 2020 with the release of not just one, but two books that deal with the subject from different perspectives. One presents the Scriptural basis for God's judgment on a nation that has exposed itself to His wrath by its complicity in taking the lives of the unborn. A vigorous argument for national repentance for the sin of abortion is well in keeping with the focus of our Nordskog vision.

Our second 2020 book touching on abortion, the book you hold in your hand, is featured under the banner of a special collection within the Nordskog Publishing family of books called the Gail Grace Nordskog Collection, headed up by my dear wife, whose name it bears. She describes it as the "softer side" of NPI, and as such, it is the perfect home for this book that speaks to the great need for personal healing from the trauma of abortion.

While our other book concerns our nation, this book is intended for the individual who has been damaged by their "choice" of abortion and needs help processing guilt, grief, and related emotions. Here, we are invited to sit together as friends and share a cup of tea, as you work through the effects abortion has had on your life. It might seem like a woman's book, but it has a message for you men as well. This book is down home, real, and intimate, coming from an author who has been through those dark woods and come out the other side with joy of life. She was able find peace and healing because of the one and only Mediator between God and man, Jesus Christ.

Dear Reader, step forth on this journey with confidence that you will encounter the One whose love for you is the healing power that will overcome any damage you have suffered.

How much more shall the blood of Christ which through the eternal Spirit offered Himself without fault to God, purge your conscience from dead works, to serve the living God? And for this cause is He the Mediator of the new Testament, that through death which was for the redemption of the transgressions that were in the former Testament, they which were called, might receive the promise of eternal inheritance. (Hebrews 9:14–15)

And you hath He quickened, that were dead in trespasses and sins, Wherein, in times past ye walked, according to the course of this world, and after the prince that ruleth in the air, even the spirit, that now worketh in the children of disobedience, Among whom we also had our conversation in time past in the lusts of our flesh, in fulfilling the will of the flesh, and of the mind, and were by nature the children of wrath, as well as others. But God which is rich in mercy, through His great love wherewith He loved us, Even when we were dead by sins, hath quickened us together in Christ, by whose grace ye are saved, And hath raised us up together, and made us sit together in the heavenly places in Christ Jesus, That He might show in the ages to come the exceeding riches of His grace through His kindness toward us in Christ Jesus. (Ephesians 2:1–7)

Wilt Thou not turn again and quicken us, that Thy people may rejoice in Thee? (Psalm 85:6)

GERALD CHRISTIAN NORDSKOG
July Fourth, Independence Day, 2020

an open door

Where I live, February is a month of promise. The rains of winter transform the brown hills into a brilliant green, and the cherry trees begin to bud. I stepped into the month of February in the year 2013 with hopefulness, but my story took an unexpected turn when three unwelcome guests took up residency in my life. Their arrival caused the green hills to fade from my view, as they captured me and took over every bit of my world. They were a constant presence in my life, so I named them Dogged-Death, Piercing-Loss, and Drawn-Out-Grieving.

Let me explain what happened. First, a dear friend of mine died. He was a very important figure in my life as a mentor and one who helped shape my worldview. He became ill and was hospitalized. I did not know how serious his condition was, but I was suddenly filled with an impulse to go to him in the hospital to take care of some unfinished business between us. I wanted to ask his forgiveness for some thoughtless behavior I had displayed. I also wanted to thank him for his mentoring over the course of our nine-year friendship. I wanted his blessing. When I got to the hospital he graciously forgave me, accepted my thanks, and gave me his blessing. We talked and sang together, and, a few days later, he passed.

While his death came as a shock to many who knew him, its impact on my life was softened somewhat by the peace and closure I experienced from our last visit together in the hospital. I found

1

it noteworthy that another friend of ours, who did not perceive the urgency and did not see him in his last days, suffered from his death much more than I did. Finding closure took longer for her than it did for me, because of those last few meaningful words I was able to share with him.

This was the first death I was to face in 2013, but not the last. Mere months later, my father died of cancer. Fifty-three days after his death, my mother died of cancer. Though they were divorced for forty-seven years, Mom and Dad received the same diagnosis at the same time and rapidly declined, as though connected by an invisible thread. My husband and I cared for each of them in their final days. We served them in their dying.

After Mom and Dad died, we held two beautiful memorial services, one for each of them. For my mother's memorial service, my sister and I took great care in preparing a table at the memorial to look just like the table in Mom's dining room—the center of her life. We covered it with her familiar Guatemalan textiles, placed her cup of coffee and croissant alongside the *New York Times* crossword puzzle, characteristically all filled in. Beside that were her jar of artist brushes, a selection of charcoal pencils, and her familiar sketchbook. We scattered photos of her beloved great-grandchildren, just as we might have found them on her table. We finished off by adding a half-eaten package of Viennese wafers, her favorite. The table was a tribute to Mom, and it brought a smile of recognition to all who knew and loved her and spent time with her at her table.

For Dad's memorial service, I composed a list of wisdom nuggets gleaned from him over my lifetime. I managed to capture his special humor as I read them aloud to the guests. Lots of people came and shared stories, laughed, and wept at both memorials, all in appropriate public expression of love and honoring that helped everyone say their goodbyes.

As time went on, I found that my grieving process continued in many different ways. It involved honoring the memories of three beloved people who lived long lives marked by dreams fulfilled, achievements, and relationships—some relationships that weathered every storm, others that were fractured beyond repair. All three were linked to me by years of history. I sorted through their belongings, cried, took long walks, wrote cathartic poems, curled up in my husband's lap, and listened to music that touched a private place of sadness. I forgave past hurts and gradually came to terms with their absence. Mostly, I poured out my sorrow to the One who gives life and knows the count of our days. He shared the burden of my lament.

Sometimes the realization of death's finality would punch me in the gut and I would struggle for my breath. Then that moment would pass, mercifully, leaving me mystified by the rare glimpse of human mortality. I was able to go on with my life in peace, with closure.

At the heart of the honoring of these dear people's lives was an assumption that they mattered. Their lives were worthy of tribute. They were known and beloved. As I considered their contributions to the world they left behind, I had some questions. I couldn't help wondering how I will be remembered and honored when I pass away. What is a person's worth? Where does our value come from? Is it all about leaving behind a legacy of great works—in the case of both my parents, studios full of artwork? What if we do nothing of note with our lives? Or what if no one knew us? Would we still be entitled to some honor? Would we still be beloved? Would we still have value?

I am sharing with you about these deaths and what I experienced during that difficult year in order to make a comparison. Many years before I lost my dear mentor and my parents, I experienced a different sort of loss. For this other one that was lost, I heard no diagnosis. The life lived by this one was not in any way noteworthy. I shared very little history with this one. I had no memories of her. We had no issues to clear up. She had no belongings for me to sort through. She had no accomplishments for me to reflect on, no dreams fulfilled, no deepened or fractured relationships. She never did anything to me that needed forgiving. There was no lifetime of successes and failures, no song, no poem, no Viennese wafers, no list of nuggets of wisdom to share with others, no birthday to remember. She was not honored with any memorial service. No one spoke of her. I did not care for her in her final days. When she died, I had no idea who she was. I didn't even consider that I had cause for grief in the case of this loss.

From such a description, you might think this other person who died had no connection to me at all. Yet she (and of course I don't really know if this person was a she or a he) spent her entire brief life inside my body, dwelling in the most intimate part of my anatomy. She was my very own child. While the deaths of my parents and my dear friend opened the door to a process of grief and gradual healing, the death of this other one brought me down blind alleys and closed doors. I plunged into a decades-long wandering through a miry darkness of guilt, shame, self-condemnation, and confusion—and mostly silence. Decades after the loss occurred, I was still no further along in processing it than when it first happened.

The loss I have just described took place when I had an abortion. With other deaths, I could travel well-worn avenues of grief processing with the help of booklets, phone calls with hospice staff, late-night conversations with my sister, condolences offered by all, and the comfort of the Jewish Mourner's Kaddish, a recitation used in the Jewish faith that speaks of God's eternal qualities. But in the case of my aborted child I couldn't find the door to a healthy grieving process. I didn't know how to understand what happened and had no way to process the shock of it.

Not only did I miss out on grieving, but I was also burdened with guilt for the part I played in my child's death. I was angry at myself and those who influenced me to take such action. The story of my abortion was complex, and there was a lot to untangle. How could I make sense of it? Would it just hang there like a dark cloud over my whole life? Would there ever come a time when I could be free of it and find peace and healing?

If you have had an abortion, perhaps you are experiencing, as I did, a disconnected, lonely, and confusing grieving process. Maybe you wouldn't even call it a grieving process—it's more of a thicket of brambles spreading its weedy tentacles into every facet of your life. Perhaps your relationships all seem to be resonating with some barely audible song of death that spoils anything that might become good. Perhaps you are walking through a perpetual foggy day, or suffer bouts of stinging guilt or melancholy, or avoid friends and family who are having children, or won't allow your dog to be a dog because you need it to be your baby, or any of a million other manifestations of unease.

However your abortion is affecting your life, how might you benefit from intentionally walking through a grieving process? Can you imagine finally finding peace and healing? Is it possible the fog of confusion is preventing you from seeing a bigger, truer picture of redemption and even joy? Could a closer look bring you out of the fog and into clarity?

We cannot expect to move forward from the hurt of abortion if the doors to an appropriate grieving process are shut. The doors might be shut by our surrounding culture that is unable to acknowledge just how traumatic abortion is. We might be singing that same old song ourselves—"It was no big deal, really." "All my girlfriends have done it, and they all seem okay." "It was a long time ago. I've left it behind." The doors to healing might be shut by the shame over what was done and the inability to look at it squarely in the face or take responsibility—by a desire to bury the experience before we have understood it. Maybe the relationships involved are just too painful to think about. Who wants to stir up a bunch of muck? What good does it do to open the floodgate of tears? Why revisit that regrettable mess? You have so many excellent and persuasive reasons *not* to seek peace and healing.

But what if a new hope were offered to you? A hope for new ways of seeing the value of your life, a new way of loving others and loving your lost child, a new way of leaving behind the crippling guilt, a new help in carrying the burden of what you've done? What if you found an open door? I ask you to hold out hope that there may be relief in store for you. When you take even a tiny step, you gain a new perspective. You can look back at where you've been, because you're not there anymore. I'd be willing to bet that—even just having read this little bit of the book you hold in your hand—you can already sense movement. When you act bravely, life might just reward you with insight and a new sense of direction. If you're stuck, you might just get unstuck. Maybe you'll inch one step closer to closure. Maybe you'll be able to put guilt, shame, and self-condemnation behind you and just grieve the loss of your child without that extra baggage darkening your outlook. Or maybe you'll be completely transformed by the blessed release of a terrible weight you have been carrying for a long time. The story of what got you to this point is uniquely your own, and the story of how you move forward will also be uniquely your own.

I don't know what lies in store for you, but I am here to help. The intent of this book is to open that door to a process that will allow you to heal and grieve. It offers a ten-part path designed to take you from the hurt of abortion to peace. What you get out of it probably depends a lot on what you put in. I offer you no guarantees, but at the very least, *Prepare a Room* will give you ideas to make things better. And the best-case scenario? You will find a whole new life.

an open door

7

"Are you willing to be changed completely, Much-Afraid, and to be made like the new name which you will receive if you become a citizen in the Kingdom of Love?"
She nodded her head and then said very earnestly, "Yes, I am."[1]

Hello, friend. The door is open—please come in and sit down. I've built a fire in the fireplace. Let me pour you some tea. I love to make my own tea blends out of the tastiest organic ingredients. I've made a special blend for you today. Do you smell the lavender? That's from my garden.

Let's talk. You are reading this book because you've been touched in some way by abortion. This book is about you. Be encouraged! I can tell you that peace, insight, healing, and comfort

---

1. The quotes at the beginning of each chapter are all taken from Hannah Hurnard's *Hind's Feet on High Places*, an allegorical story in which a character named Much-Afraid goes on a long journey of transformation from the Valley of Humiliation to the High Places, where she receives a new name and a new life. This is my hope for you. (Blacksburg, VA: Wilder Publications, 2010).

can be found—I know this because I have found relief, and I know others who have as well.

You are brave—this is a touchy subject, and it takes courage to examine one's life choices. Yet that very courage is what opens the door to peace and healing. You have overcome the impulse to run away and push these memories deep down. You are willing to revisit old hurts in the hopes of getting to the bottom of the unease inside of you. In walking through this door, you are going against the currents of our culture that tell you there is no reason to hurt from abortion. You may be also be going against messages you've received from friends, family, or community. I'm already so proud of you.

This book will present a step-by-step path to come to terms with what is a very difficult chapter of your life. Here you will find no judgment or rejection, because I don't consider myself any better than you—who am I to judge, after what I have done? We're in the same boat in many ways. Here you will find respect, honesty, practical advice, spiritual guidance, teachings to help you grow, and new ways of thinking about how to move forward. Throughout this process, your unique experience will be honored. You will be asked to answer questions and reflect on things, and for that purpose I have left you spaces in each chapter where you can write. Go grab your pen or pencil and keep it ready. Take your time—I have enough tea to last as long as we need.

All Are Welcome Here

Although this book is primarily for women who have had one or more abortions, it may also be a help to men and to friends or family members touched by abortion. You may be the grandma that didn't get to be a grandma because of your child's decision. You may be the happily married man looking back at thoughtless teenage choices. You may be the one who took your doctor's advice and aborted your Down's syndrome child. You may be the young person caught in the cycle of using abortion as a form of birth control. You may be the sister who did nothing as you watched someone you love make a terrible decision. You may have been forced to get an abortion against your wishes. All our stories are different. There's something here for everyone.

The effects of abortion ripple through families and communities, even if it is not spoken of. It also ripples through time. For some this is fresh stuff, for others it reaches back many years or even decades. You may be young or old, of any race, nationality, economic level, or religion. You may be homeless, or you may be living a very comfortable life. You may be one person tackling this alone, or you may be part of a women's group, church study group, or cluster of close friends working on this topic together.

Because you are all so very different from one another, each with a unique story and in a unique phase of life, the material you will find in this book will probably apply to you very fittingly in some places and less fittingly in others. Some discussions will be more relevant to you, and others, less so. That is to be expected when dealing with a topic that touches such a broad range of circumstances. In 12-step programs they have a saying: "Take what you like and leave the rest." Stay on the path and I'm certain some part of what you find here will make a difference for each of you.

If you are using this book in a group, be sure to respect each member of the group for her unique story and needs. Keep your focus on your own path, and how you can be a help and support to the others in the group. Be worthy of the trust others place in you. Be thoughtful. Be sure to make time for everyone who wishes to speak. All members of the group do not have to be working on the same chapter at the same time. Allow each person to go at her own pace. Honor confidentiality and treat one another with gentleness. However you use this book, take small steps—remember you are treading into deep waters.

If you are using this book alone and have no one to speak to, my heart goes out to you. Maybe I can be an encouragement to you through these pages, like that elder auntie who listens and doesn't want to see you hurting. You really are not alone. Others have walked this path and come out the other side.

Imagining Rooms

As we proceed through these chapters, I am going to ask you to think conceptually. You may have been wondering what it means to "prepare a room." No, I'm not going to ask you to go to Bed, Bath, and Beyond. Preparing a room isn't about interior decorating—it is a thought exercise. You have real rooms in the house where you live—a bedroom, living room, and kitchen. They each have a unique purpose. Now, for a moment, let's imagine that your life is a kind of house with various rooms for different purposes. You might have a room in your life's house for your relationship with your parents, one for your work life, one for your health, one for your spiritual walk, and so on. We are going to imagine three new rooms in your life's house. As you move through these chapters, you can claim these three rooms as your own and develop them as useful tools of healing.

The word *prepare* comes from Latin meaning "to put in a state of readiness." Preparing a room is a way of saying, "I want to be in a state of readiness for my healing process. It takes priority in my life right now. It is worthy of my time and attention. I will give it the space it deserves."

Let me give an example of what I mean. Occasionally, my sister visits me. In preparing for her visits, I vacuum, put fresh sheets on her bed, and cut some flowers from the garden to add delight to her space. I go through these preparations because she is important and deserves to be treated with care and love. Similarly, you will prepare these imaginary rooms, because your healing process is important and deserves to be treated with care and love.

As we move through this process, you will see more and more clearly how to make the most of this thought exercise for your healing. It will be a way of honoring yourself, your child, and the God who created you both.

The "rooms" you will prepare are figurative, not literal. The work of "preparing a room" takes place inside your mind and heart. It's all about your attitude, attention, and willingness to go through the process.

Foundational Ideas

Abortion is a hot-button political issue. You can go on the Internet and find plenty of debate on the topic. You can find statistics about abortion, as well as detailed descriptions of the processes involved. You can even find unspeakably horrid photos of the tiny victims. You won't find those things here. They do not further the pursuit of peace and healing. Along the way, I will share some of my ideas about destructive strains I see in today's society that influence us, but I will bring out these points only insofar as they touch on your healing. I want to help you, not engage in political debate. Our decisions are not made in a vacuum, so we do need to see how our culture has urged us along. That way, we can reevaluate our assumptions and start to think for ourselves.

Let me tell you a little about where I'm coming from. I wrote this book because I care very much about you. The purpose of this book is to be a help to you, and part of that help means breaking down some of the lies told in today's society. Believing those lies may be part of what got you where you are today, and recognizing them will help you move on to a better place. I am not neutral about what is best for you. Some of what passes for normal in the culture today is really not good for you, so it needs to be talked about. I hold strong ideas not only about breaking down lies, but about building up truth. Yes, there is such a thing as truth, and our alliance with truth ensures our victory over lies and the damage done by them.

I start with the understanding that we human beings are made by God, and he has placed within us a moral compass that informs us of right and wrong. You could call it your conscience. Our wrong actions go against that inner moral compass, causing us guilt and grief. Furthermore, our wrong actions fracture our relationship with God—the One who placed the sense of right and wrong inside us so that we would choose right over wrong. We must not be afraid to say that abortion is wrong. Our built-in morality tells us so, though some have willingly abandoned their moral compass and cannot see clearly to make such an admission.

All our actions in life are either taking us on a path toward the right—toward the positive, toward wholesomeness, beauty, joy, life, and thriving—or they are taking us on a path toward the wrong—toward the negative, toward darkness, destruction, waste, death, and ugliness. When we head toward where God is, we find all that is good and life giving, and when we turn away from God, that negative stuff takes over and we suffer its ill effects. Abortion took us down the wrong road and made death a part of our story. The trick is to turn around and head toward God. He helps us find life, even in the midst of death.

What about the children lost in abortion? I approach this topic with the understanding that abortion takes the life of a living human being—not "non-specific tissue," not a "potential" human, not an inconvenience, not a parasite, not a punishment, not a clump of cells, but a human being. Sometimes we hear the words *embryo* and *fetus* used to minimize the humanity of the child in the womb. Yet those words very clearly speak of a living human being in development. What does *Merriam-Webster Dictionary* say about these words that are intended to distance us from the presence of life in the womb? The dictionary defines *embryo* as a "developing human individual," and *fetus* as "a developing human." Saying, "It was just an *embryo*," or, "It was only a *fetus*," doesn't excuse taking a life. He or she was a developing human individual. There is no room here for "your truth" and "my truth" here. The only truth is that the child developing in the womb is indeed a human being.

We are all endowed with intrinsic value as human beings. This is true of our unborn children, and it is also true of us. Our lives have meaning that arises from the full expression of love—the love we give, but even more, the love we are given by God, the source of life, our Creator. Our identity is found in relation to him, from whose love we derive our great worth. We are beloved by him and have been created with purpose, not as random accidents. So often, we try to concoct some value for our lives based on our own changeable ideas, deeds, or moods. These tend to fall short when they come up against a serious challenge to our self-worth, such as we are presented with in the case of abortion. By contrast, our value that is rooted in our Creator's love for us is unchanging, unshakable, and absolutely solid under any circumstances we might face.

If you don't believe in God, or if you have questions or doubts in that area, *you are especially welcome here.* You are actually the one I was thinking of when I wrote this book. I have tried to speak to you in as genuine a manner as I can—just as one person to another—as equals sharing a pot of tea together at the table. You are encouraged to stick around and see if something in these pages resonates with you.

Face to Face

Crystal is a young woman about twenty-three years of age, stylish and lovely, with wavy black hair and beautiful brown eyes.[2] She was deeply alarmed as she watched her relationship with her boyfriend fall apart because of her uncontrolled raging, and she called our local pregnancy center for help. She had begun to suspect that her problems were somehow connected with her two abortions. I was asked to reach out to her to see if she wanted to meet and talk. She was eager to meet, but it took a long time to pin her down for an actual appointment.

Finally, we were able to arrange a meeting. She sat across the picnic table from me in a remote corner of a public park. We were shaded from the summer heat by eucalyptus trees towering overhead. Her eyes continually darted toward the shouts of young people clustered by the baseball field not far away. She seemed concerned that someone might see her and recognize her. I waited for her to collect herself. We were silent for some time. Finally she faced me, her shoulders fell in resignation, and she started to cry.

---

2. Most names in this book have been changed to preserve anonymity.

Sitting across the picnic table from me that day, Crystal shared about her multiple abortion experiences and how she felt they were affecting her life. I could see how much courage it took to make these very personal admissions. I mostly listened, as a friend or caring auntie would do, and I offered feedback when appropriate. At the end of an hour's meeting, Crystal was delightfully unburdened. She seemed immune to the law of gravity as she flew over to me and swooped me into a hug. She thanked me with tears and a big smile and asked if we could meet weekly because she got so much out of this first meeting. We made plans and parted. Crystal clearly benefited from our meeting. We connected. She was willing to make commitments in an effort to control her rage and to take on an assignment to help her think differently about her behaviors. We parted on a hopeful note.

In the next few weeks, Crystal and I texted and made followup dates. But there was always a reason on her end why those dates couldn't take place. She had scheduling conflicts, made last-minute cancellations, and, after a few months of checking in by text and missing opportunities to meet, she stopped responding altogether. I haven't seen Crystal since that meeting in the park.

Maybe that was all the help that Crystal needed. Maybe she just needed a kick-start to set her on a positive path, and once she got that, she was good to go. Maybe she found help elsewhere and is now on a positive trajectory, free of the troubles that brought her to make that first phone call. Or maybe Crystal wanted so badly to be done thinking about an unpleasant part of her life that one meeting was all she could handle. Maybe she'll revisit these issues in twenty years. Maybe not. I don't know.

Unfortunately, in my experience, avoidance behavior is not unusual among women in need of help to cope with their abortions. They cry out for help, so desperate in the moment, but, often, as soon as you reach out to them, they recoil. They show initial interest, and then you never hear from them again. They don't return calls. They cancel appointments. They don't show up.

Another reaction I have come to expect occurs when I speak publicly on the topic of abortion. I often encounter a dazed, frozen audience. The women hold very still, like I'm a T-Rex, and I won't see them if they don't move a muscle. They slip away quickly so they won't have to talk to me. I guess it must be that I'm super scary, right? Or maybe people just don't have a convenient compartment in their brains for this deeply scarred part of their lives. The awful thing happened, and then it got shoved to the bottom of the trash bin where no one will dig it up. Hearing it spoken of in public is like having your used sanitary pads hung on display. It's simply horrifying and offensive. Even the suggestion that there is something there worth talking about is strange and ugly and entirely new.

After my experience with Crystal, I began to wonder if there might be another way to help hurting women work through the particularly thorny issues surrounding abortion. What if you could pursue a self-directed path to peace and healing on your own time, at your own pace, and in the privacy of your own home?

Thanks to Crystal, *Prepare a Room* was born. It was conceived as a self-paced help that allows for personal space and privacy in the grieving and healing process. It grows out of my own experience of what has helped me in finding peace and healing from my years of emotional fallout from abortion.

You will hear me speak of finding peace and of finding healing. I use these two words to differentiate two distinct areas of wounding that I see in people who are hurt by abortion. We need to grieve the loss of our children, and we need relief from guilt, shame, and the damage done to our identity by our decisions. When we allow the grieving process to have full expression, we are on the road to peace. When we look deeply at our identity issues, we are on the road to healing. These two strains intersect and get tangled in confusing ways. Both will be addressed as we go along our ten-step path. I see peace and healing ahead for you. What does that look like? It looks like a life of freedom, joy, and acceptance, with laughter mixed in there with the tears. It looks like a whole life lived in full sunlight instead of a half-lived subsistence spent hiding in darkness.

I am not a professional or licensed counselor or therapist. I have no credentials to bring to the table in presenting this help. I am trained as an animator, I've owned businesses, and I currently work as an editor. My areas of expertise from years of doing many varied things are miles away from the field of psychology. But I have the advantage of having dug some deep, ugly holes for myself that I had to climb out of, so you can benefit from my mistakes. What I bring is common sense, a God-given desire to help, compassion for you, and experience with abortion—both my own and from working with others in workshops and one on one. I did not learn the ideas in this book in college programs or counselor training sessions, from books, or on YouTube. This ten-step path comes out of my life experience and what I think will best help you.

Sometimes a book just isn't enough. If you need to speak to someone in person, I encourage you to find resources in your area and reach out to pastors, rabbis, elders, licensed counselors, or trusted friends for face-to-face help. If you are thinking of harming yourself, immediately call 911 or the National Suicide Prevention Lifeline at 1-800-273-TALK (8255).

Other Voices

Let me put another log on the fire. Now that we've gotten acquainted, I'd like you to know there are other people rooting for you. You'll be hearing from these and others from time to time as we move forward. Like me, they already care so much about you!

Let's hear from Melissa...

I initially received the message that nothing is wrong with abortion and therefore you have no cause to be hurting from it. Now I believe that until you really examine the experience you never "deal" with it. I would like to help others to not make the same mistake I made.

Let's hear from Tammy...

I feel so concerned for the girls that are being urged into activities that hurt them. I want to just tell them to think before they act. These decisions about pregnancy have lifelong consequences. It's hard to see that, particularly when you're young.

Let's hear from Beth...

I hope each of you finds a way to get set free from your past abortion stories. I hope that each of you can forgive yourselves and cling to God for freedom from the pain and trauma you face at this time of remorse, guilt, and anger.

Let's hear from Jim...

I encourage you, dear Reader, to dig into this book, and do it with the expectation of having a reinforcement of your self worth and a way to understand this trauma that you experienced. Relief and a sense of peace can come from examining, coming to grips with, and owning the experience.

Let's hear from Rose...

Many men and women are hurt and grieving after they have an abortion, even those who believe in their "right to choose." Beyond the political, there are people who are sad, and this book addresses this sadness and gives hope and healing.

Here are some questions to help you get started:

※ What has brought you to a willingness to look more closely at your abortion experience?

※ Is your willingness mixed with reluctance?

※ What do you think you might gain from a closer look at your abortion experience?

Prepare a Room

2 prepare a room

Though the uproar of the tempest without was almost deafening and the hut shuddered and shook in every blast, yet inside was nothing but peace and thanksgiving and cheerful contentment.

I recently watched a documentary about Magnus Carlsen, a young chess phenom who challenged the top chess master for the title of World Chess Champion in Chennai, India, in 2013. The psychological pressure on these two competitors as they matched brainpower was unimaginable. To isolate the players from any interference from outside their match, a special room was constructed. It was a small, soundproof chamber with a glass front, designed with the sole purpose of securing an environment within which the two chess rivals could concentrate without distraction.

These chess-match rooms have been described as "a double-layered, glass-enclosed 'fish tank'," resembling "a large museum display case with one-way glass so spectators can see in but the players cannot see out."[1] In the room are a table and two chairs, the chessboard, a timer, pens and paper for taking notes, and water to drink. That's all the competitors need to play the game. They sit, they think, they make a move at the chessboard, they take a sip of water, they write a note, they get up and stretch, and they sit back down at the board.

The space just on the other side of the one-way glass, unseen by the players, is teeming with spectators and the media—photographers with their cameras snapping away at a furious pace, practically falling over each other to capture every change of facial expression, every move, every moment. Yet, the players cannot hear them or see them. A world of commotion may be exploding mere inches away from them, but their special room is insulated from interference. It's absolutely quiet in their space. They are able to perform at the very highest level of their game without being disturbed or interrupted. These extreme measures are taken out of respect for the game and the players.

Just as the chess players need a quiet place, so too, you are invited to construct your own special place to concentrate on your healing. As I said in the last chapter, during the course of the chapters of this book, you will be asked to conceive of a room. In fact, you will prepare three imaginary, conceptual rooms, special spaces for healing to occur. These are not real rooms, but a way of "making room" in your life for this very important process. The first room you are invited to imagine is a room for you. It is to be a secure space in what will probably be a season of increased sensitivity as you uncover and explore difficult feelings about your abortion.

What does it mean to prepare a room that isn't a literal room? How is that done?

Let's start with the walls. The chess-championship chamber had walls that were designed to keep out distraction and allow for

1. Leon Watson, "World Chess to probe mystery noise in soundproof game room," *Evening Standard* (November 20, 2018), standard.co.uk.

concentration. You are looking for a space—and that space has everything to do with your focus, determination, and attitude—that keeps out distraction and interruption so you can concentrate on the task ahead of you. Outside your room may be a world of commotion in the form of turbulent relationships, loved ones whose needs tug at you, and the million things that cry out to be attended to in any given day. Are there ways you can place some boundaries around the unique needs of this moment? Can you lighten your daily tasks in order to make time for this healing project? What can you do to dial down stress in difficult relationships at this time? Are you able to tell those around you that you need some extra margin right now as you process difficult life issues? Is there a regular time each week that you can set aside to devote to this process?

The chess masters didn't need much in their room. What do you need in your room? Yourself. If the chess competitors don't show up for their match, they forfeit the game to their opponent. You don't want to forfeit your game. You need to be present for your own challenge. Can you commit to braving the hurt and not running away from it? You're going to be digging deep during this process. Along the way, you will discover what sustains you and what distracts you. Don't allow "shiny objects" to seduce you away from a deeper calling to true healing.

Having said that, be sure you have some practical tools, such as a notebook and pencil or tablet, in case the space for writing in this book is not enough. You might wish to leave Facebook and Instagram and such outside your room.

Who was allowed in the chess room? The only ones allowed in the chess room were the players and a few trusted people for security. You are beginning to look deeply into your abortion experience. Is there anyone you can trust to share about it? This should be someone who won't minimize your feelings and who will respect your confidentiality. Use wisdom in deciding which people to share with and which people not to share with. There may be those you need to exclude. Find a loving and gentle way to do so—they don't even need to know what you're doing. You don't want to create new problems while you're working out old ones.

If you are part of a group of people going through this process together, start out by discussing the importance of confidentiality. You want to be able to wholly trust one another, as you are allowing one another access to your rooms. The qualities you should bring to such a group are those you would like to see others display toward you: gentleness, kindness, patience, respect, thoughtfulness, and the ability to speak the truth with love.

Here's a further idea for you: I urge you to invite God into the room you are preparing. As I make this suggestion, I'm reminded of the time Moses led the Jewish people as they fled from the Pharaoh in Egypt, where they were slaves. Behind them was Pharaoh's army closing in on them, and in front of them was the Red Sea. The people were stuck, as it were, between a rock and a hard place. They didn't know God. They didn't have any reason to trust God to deliver them. But Moses encouraged them:

> Fear not, stand firm, and see the salvation of the LORD, which he will work for you today.... The LORD will fight for you, and you have only to be silent."[2]

Then God parted the Red Sea, and the people escaped by walking through the sea as on dry land. Moses's message is for you today. Read it over and take it personally. Maybe you don't know God yet either. Maybe you don't have any reason to trust him. But just stand back and see what he will do for you. Be encouraged with the thought that if you invite God in, he may surprise you with your own sort of parted-waters deliverance from bondage to guilt and regret.

What took place in the chess room? The chess room was dedicated to one activity, and that activity was the most important thing in that space. Your room will be dedicated to your healing

---

2. Exodus 14:13–14 ESV.

process. Keep your focus on the project at hand. Problems are like bunnies—they have a way of multiplying. You may start out with one focus, but because you just had to say such-and-such to so-and-so, suddenly now you have a compounded problem. Before you know it, the original purpose of healing from abortion has become a big mess of interpersonal strife. Then you're left with the chore of untangling more knots, and you've lost your concentration. Other problems can wait for another day.

Strong feelings may arise, and you may be tempted to act on them. This is not the time to lash out—that is just another distraction. Best not to act on your feelings now. You have plenty of time in the future when your raw feelings have been tempered by the passage of time, healing, and thoughtful consideration. Chapter 10, Point of Departure, discusses actions you might take moving forward after you've gone through this process. But that's for the future, not for now.

The chess players respected each other. The players met in their special room, each knowing that the other was worthy of the highest regard. So too, you are worthy of the highest regard, and your healing process is to be honored by you and all you let into your room—that is, all you let into your confidence as you go through this. Let your room be a place of love. Bring compassion for all involved. Recognize that you are embarking on something that may completely change all your relationships for the better.

Some of you may think I'm belaboring this point about preparing a room. You already know how to work through your feelings and examine yourself. You don't have to be told to keep a journal. Maybe you've been through therapy or attended support groups. You're a self-help pro. But you have not considered until very recently that your experience in this particular area is worthy of deep reflection. For those, I say, bring all the tools in your tool belt to this project. Now is the time to make a place in your life to honor this particular challenge.

Give your room some thought. Here are some questions to help you conceive of it:

☀ Can you commit to a dedicated time each week for concentration on this healing process? Are you willing to "show up" for it?

☀ What challenges will you face in trying to make space in your life for this healing journey? How can you manage these challenges so they don't keep you from moving forward?

☀ How would you describe your room?

Prepare a Room

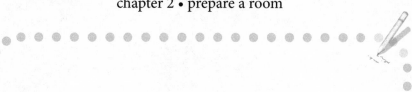

3 time to stop

For hours poor Much-Afraid lay sleepless on her bed, too bruised in mind and body to rest in one position, but tossing and turning wearily from side to side until long after midnight. Somewhere at the back of her mind was a dreadful uneasiness, as though there was something she ought to remember, but was unable to do so.

Once, when I was a young mother, I had to have a tooth extracted. During my recovery time, I began to sketch an imaginary character that popped into my mind and seemed to insist on coming to life. I was trained as an animator, and I loved to visualize characters to animate. This particular one was a tiny little girl with black pigtails. I imagined that she lived alone in a wild, littered wasteland. She filled my imagination with adventures, as she invented new uses for the random broken and discarded trash that surrounded her—stuff like old bicycle parts and bent television antennas. She wore a skirt made from leaves. I drew her and wrote little stories from her point of view. She had a talent for making good and useful things out of garbage. And she had an indomitably cheerful countenance in spite of being an orphan all alone. She was a delightful companion, though I never completed any cartoons that featured her. She was just there, just a hobby I played with on the side. She always seemed to have the same message for me: "I have a story to tell, but I know you're not ready to hear it. One day maybe, my story will be told."

It took many years for me to recognize who this patient little girl—this orphan child living among discarded things—really represented. When I suddenly realized that she was a place saver for my little one lost in abortion, I was shocked and overwhelmed with tearful astonishment. How could I be so blind as to not see who she was? I was amazed at the depth of my need for connection with—and yet unawareness of—what was lost. Somebody seemingly much smarter than my conscious self was working below the surface of my understanding to dream up this method of keeping her near, but not too near. My little imaginary friend served to shield me from the horror of loss and was instead a comforting presence. She stood by me for years, and when I was ready to face it—even though it took a long time—she was right there with what seemed like forgiveness and acceptance that soothed my guilt. After all, she was practiced at turning broken stuff into good things.

Some experiences are just too hurtful to face. We bury our hurts, but they have a way of popping back up. You've heard of Post Traumatic Stress Syndrome. PTSD occurs when a terrifying experience traumatizes a person, causing uncontrollable thoughts, nightmares, anxiety, and a host of other symptoms. The Mayo Clinic says,

> Post-traumatic stress disorder symptoms may start within one month of a traumatic event, but sometimes symptoms may not appear until years after the event. These symptoms cause significant problems in social or work situations and in relation-

ships. They can also interfere with your ability to go about your normal daily tasks.[1]

Psychologists have also identified a stress disorder unique to those traumatized by abortion. It is called Post Abortion Stress Syndrome (PASS). Yet, oddly, when you read the articles about PASS that can be found online, the writers seem to be driven more than anything to pound home the idea that PASS doesn't exist. You see this even in the title of a *Psychology Today* article: "Post Abortion Stress Syndrome (PASS)—Does It Exist?"[2] The same people who acknowledge the impact of combat trauma apparently wish to minimize the impact of an invasive procedure that destroys a life within the most intimate part of a woman's anatomy.

The current culture is inconvenienced by the presence of post-abortion trauma. This may even be true of some individuals in your circle of friends or family. They would rather it didn't exist. The culture of denial ties in with our healing challenge, because we don't find compassion or encouragement when we seek help; instead, we are urged to enter into denial ourselves.

Some of us even encounter hostility when we speak of our hurts from abortion. I was shocked and dismayed to hear of the backlash experienced by the unique and inspired photographer Angela Forker, who describes her work as "allowing women and men to express the pain they've experienced after an abortion through conceptual photography—while also focusing on the healing that can be found."

Let's hear from Angela...

For the most part, these photos are received in an overwhelmingly positive manner. Women and men write to me from all over the world, thanking me for the healing they've found! On several occasions, however, my page has been maliciously attacked by people who do not agree that

1. "Post-traumatic stress disorder (PTSD)," Mayo Clinic, mayoclinic.org.
2. Susanne Babbel, "Post Abortion Stress Syndrome (PASS)—Does It Exist?" *Psychology Today* (October 25, 2010), psychologytoday.com.

post-abortive women and men might suffer great pain and regret after their abortion. Some of my posts have been posted in pro-choice and feminist groups, calling everyone to come onto my page to ridicule the women and men in my photos. They have mocked, insulted, and even made fun of my photography. They also claimed this was fake news.

The harassment sometimes seems too difficult to bear, but I know that I must continue to allow post-abortive women and men to have a voice, especially when their voice is making such a great difference. My photo series is helping many find healing and is helping prevent others from making a choice that could haunt them the rest of their lives.[3]

A general climate of hostility is part of the reason we find ourselves with deep wounds that go untended, in some cases for years. Our first task is to disengage from the culture of denial. No, you're not crazy to feel what you feel. Don't let anyone minimize what you're going through. These contrary voices need to shut down the conversation in order to bolster their irrational argument arising from a sickness of their hearts. Whether or not PASS exists is a question I will leave for you to decide for yourself. For our purposes, let's proceed with the understanding that, even if we don't call it a syndrome or give it a name, abortion is a traumatic event that has left its mark on our lives in unexpected ways, not unlike PTSD.

The Irrational Hulk

Do you ever feel like you're two people? One minute you're under control and life is going along normally, then the next minute you're triggered by some little incident, and you transform into someone you don't recognize? Your feelings explode all out of proportion to the circumstance, and you transform into the Irrational Hulk, a giant, green monster intent on destruction. You

---

3. Check out Angela Forker at aftertheabortion.com. Read about her work at humandefense.com/after-the-abortion-photography-series-depicts-real-post-abortive-emotions/. Contact her at preciousbabyphotography@outlook.com.

tromp all over the tiny people of the village, flip over their cars, uproot trees and throw them across the landscape. And when it's all over, you barely remember, and you don't understand what happened. Who in the world is this other person?

Sometimes the strength of your feelings frightens you. You are overcome with shame, or seemingly inappropriate grief, or burning resentment. Maybe you're hypersensitive and assume that others around you are disrespecting you. Or perhaps you are paralyzed by an inability to make decisions, by self-pity, self-doubt, or self-blame. One day you're okay, and the next, you can hardly find the motivation to get out of bed. Or maybe you are fine during the day, but at night the nightmares come.

Sometimes, when we bury our feelings and don't face things, we end up as the Irrational Hulk. Likewise, our everyday challenges expand and compound into a giant, irrational, hulking, green pile of problems. One way that we feed the Irrational Hulk is by indulging self-destructive behaviors. For example, if you're emotionally triggered by seeing a pregnant mom pushing a child in a stroller, you might find yourself so uncomfortable that you harm yourself in some way. You started out with one issue: emotions coming from buried feelings. But by harming yourself, you create a new problem. Remember how problems multiply like bunnies?

In the last chapter we discussed that the chess players have to show up for their own match, or else they forfeit the game. I suggested that you, in turn, need to show up for your own challenge. One way of *not* showing up for your healing process is by turning to self-destructive behaviors. Self-destructive behaviors will hinder you from finding peace and healing from abortion. Those behaviors keep us from honestly facing deeper wounds. You can't reach the buried stuff until you remove the ugly, green mess that's piled up on top of it. Self-destructive behaviors may include overeating, promiscuousness, raging, lying, irresponsibility, alcohol or drug use, cutting, or being drawn to hurtful relationships. Unprocessed wounds can cause you to act out. Your abortion may be at the root of those wounds, or it may be part of a larger complex of wounds.

The Ultimate Self-Destructive Behavior

Abortion introduces a spirit of death into our lives. That spirit of death casts a shadow over all we do and can sometimes cause us to have thoughts of suicide. If you are having these thoughts right now, put this book down and reach out to a pastor or other clergy, a trusted friend, or a licensed counselor—or call the National Suicide Prevention Lifeline at 1-800-273-TALK (8255).

But more likely, if you have gotten this far in reading, you probably have at least a glimmer of hope that things will get better. Let me assure you that peace and healing lie ahead for you, but if you succumb to these deathly thoughts, you will absolutely shut down any possibility of seeing the wrongs made right, of redeeming the lost and broken relationships—with God and with your child. Don't shut that door—you can't reopen it! Redemption is right around the corner.

Let's Hear from Alec...

I have been guilty of trying to take my own life. I am thankful that there is no suffering that is wasted in God's economy, and that all suffering of God's adopted children is redemptive at its core. By God's grace, I am able to minister to many hurting people. God is wise and good and able to use each and every one of his adopted sons and daughters, if we are only willing to be used.

When Alec speaks above of suffering as "redemptive," what does that mean? *Redemption* means that a devalued thing that was bound for the flames of the garbage heap is snatched from the fire and given new life. For Alec, *redemption* means that even his suicidal suffering has been given value. Because of the newness of life that Alec has experienced, he is now able to counsel and help others find meaning through the dark valleys of life.

Alec tells me that suicide is a permanent "solution" (i.e., not a solution at all) to a temporary problem, and that most people don't really want to take their lives so much as they want to escape an unbearable life situation. He would say that a ruined life can be snatched from the flames of destruction. You have a reason to carry on and make the effort to see how something deadly, ugly, and twisted can be redeemed and transformed into something life-giving, beautiful, and joyful.

Something that Helps

You've gone to a good deal of effort to prepare a room for healing from the hurt of abortion—did the Irrational Hulk make itself at home in the room with you? How can you start looking at your abortion experience without a bunch of extra noise confusing the topic?

If you are someone who needs to be told that these self-destructive behaviors are wrong—that it's time to stop hurting others and doing harm to yourself—well here I am, and I'm telling you, *it's time to stop.* I don't want to minimize the difficulty of stopping destructive behaviors—they have served a purpose for you, even if it's twisted, illogical, and counterproductive. They are not easy to kick. But, no excuses. I want you to be honest about what you're doing and consider the effect it's having in your life. Beyond what this book can do for you, I urge you to seek a supportive community or counselor to help you stop. The road is tough, but compassionate help is out there. Let's start today so that you can continue unhindered on your path to peace and healing from abortion.

Once upon a time, my husband and I went through a season of our marriage that was very stressful. We owned a business and had a huge warehouse and a fleet of trucks. Things went wrong sometimes. Our drivers got in accidents. We had insurance claims against us. We had trouble getting proper licensing. Money was always a problem. We were under government audit. One thing after another arose, and it created a lot of stress. I responded to the stress by creating more stress. I would explode in anger at my husband, or break something, or run away. One day, my husband said something to me that made all the difference. His simple words of wisdom have become a life motto, and I now share them with you. He said, "Do something that helps." In other words, I had a choice of how to handle the stress of my life. I could choose to respond in a way that made things worse—that added to the giant, green pile of problems—or I could choose to respond in a way that made things better. When we choose to "do something that helps," we are untangling the mess instead of making more mess. The Irrational Hulk starts to lose its destructive power.

As you look at the strategies you use to deal with stresses—some of which might be from your unresolved abortion experience—how can you "do something that helps"? Could you hold your tongue when what you have to say only makes things worse? Can you control your temper? Could you remove yourself from a volatile situation and take a time out? Can you divert your attention to a small, manageable project so that you can have the satisfaction of completing one productive task? Can you ask God to help you control your destructive thoughts? This is the sort of thinking that will help rather than hinder you.

Your Value

As I write this, I have just learned—to my horror—that a teen I care about very much has begun to cut herself. How I would love to say something to this girl that would help her stop this self-destructive behavior! Doesn't she know that her life has value? When all the voices from the culture, on TV and in movies, on the Internet and in magazines and in the classroom, reinforce the singular message that our existence is merely the result of random processes and we have no purpose—that humans beings are the problem with our planet—life becomes meaningless. We are devalued. When you think your life has no value, one action is as good as another, so—why not cut yourself? Who cares?

But wait a minute. What if we were created with intention and love? What if we do have purpose, and life does have meaning? What if we are, indeed, highly valued? Where does our value come from? I propose that our value comes from knowing deep inside that we are cherished. As you consider this, let me refresh your tea and invite you to hear a story that will illustrate this idea.

This is the story of a father who has a headstrong, rebellious daughter. She runs away from home because she wants to do what she wants and not be under her father's authority. With nothing to hold her back, she follows her desires wherever they lead. She tastes all the "forbidden fruit" she can get her hands on, yet for all the living outside the lines, the daughter's desires are never really satisfied. The things she aims for turn out to be insignificant. Those she calls friends abandon her when she comes to them with needs. Years fly by. Her money dries up, and she racks up debts she can't possibly repay. She finds only deeper and deeper degradation and emptiness. With every step further away from home, her pursuits turn more and more sour. If she keeps on this road, she knows she will die. She thinks of home and longs to go back, but by now she is sure her father is disgusted with her. She no longer feels worthy of his love. But where else can she go?

The rebellious daughter finally hits rock bottom. She comes to her senses and heads home. But the home she comes back to is very different from the one she left. The home she left was hateful to her. She thought it held her back, as though she could never fulfill her dreams there. But now, with new eyes, she sees that her dreams were made of paper and fluttered away in the wind, while home is solid and genuine. Home is where she is most completely seen and heard and known. She is cherished there and once counted that as nothing. Now, she sees that being cherished is what gives her life value. Is it possible she could still be cherished after rejecting her father so hurtfully?

Meanwhile, the father looks out the window and sees his precious daughter coming up the path, looking haggard and spent. His heart spills over with joy and relief that his daughter is finally home. Even while his child was out running wild, he never stopped loving her. Every moment she was gone, he hoped and waited for her return. To her surprise, he runs out to meet her, without even knowing her intentions in returning. For all he knows, she might be ready to deliver another hurtful slap in the face, yet he's willing to take that chance. Instead of scolding her, he sheds tears of joy over her return.

The daughter tells her father she doesn't deserve to be accepted back, because she has wasted her life. She opens up to him about all she has done. The father is deeply grieved by his daughter's degradation, but he can see that she is broken and humbled by all she's been through. Her experiences out in the world have dealt a blow to her self-worth. But, to him, she is of infinite value. He pays all her debts for her. He tells her, "You were dead, but now you're alive again. You were lost, but now you're found." She realizes then that—yes, she can be cherished again. Where once the daughter devalued her inheritance and just wanted to run from it, now she finds that the inheritance her father has for her is not what she thought it was. It is not made of material things, but it is an inheritance of love, magnificent beyond her wildest imaginings.

Now imagine that you—with all you've gone through surrounding your abortion, all that led to it, and all that followed it—you are that daughter. Yours is the spiritual and emotional bankruptcy. Yours is the unpayable debt of wrongs done. But yours also is the loving father who values you above all else. Yours is the inheritance of love. Your father has watched as you have gone through life like a lost lamb without a shepherd, and he has compassion for you born of his love for you. He made you. He grieves with you over the griefs of your life and is willing to pay any price in order to welcome you into his arms and call you his beloved. He has been patiently waiting for you to set your heart in his direction.

This story is one way to understand who God is, and how valued you are in God's eyes. Your value comes from *his high regard for you*, as his beloved child. As you move into the next chapter, where you will recount the events surrounding your abortion in great detail, hold tightly to this picture of a father's love. It is for you. Remember that you have great value, not for anything you have done or not done, but because of who he is. Even if you can't see your own value, let the love of God, your spiritual father, be your source of self-worth.

As a valued, unique, precious child of the most loving father, can you commit to stopping behaviors that are not consistent with being God's beloved daughter? Write down your commitment. It might go something like this, for example:

I make a commitment to stop stuffing my face with junk food every time I feel triggered. A beloved child of God doesn't act out that way.

I don't want alcohol in my life. Alcohol only pushes me further from the love and respect I seek.

From now on, I will no longer throw things at my husband. I will find ways to speak to him with respect. I have value, and so does he.

Smoking pot makes me stupid. My life is too valuable to throw away on pot.

I will ask God to help me.

Doing the Best You Can

While we make these commitments, I know most of us keep commitments imperfectly. But I am proud of you for being willing to make a commitment to do better. If you sometimes fall short of your goal, you can get up off the ground and start again. Instead of being discouraged, be encouraged that you put your commitment in writing. That is no small thing. By writing it down and owning it, you are starting to take hold of the situation. You are moving in a positive direction. You are no longer feeding the Irrational Hulk. Instead of compounding your problems, you are starting to untangle the mess of threads so you can separate out and identify the issues you need to address. You will need alertness and sobriety as you move forward. Keep your eye on the prize of peace and healing, and hang on to the love of God that gives your life worth.

We've taken some time to get to know one another and lay the groundwork for a thorough telling of your abortion experience. You've prepared a respectful room in which to hold your healing process. You're ready to move away from the pattern of self-destructive behaviors that masks a deeper hurt. Before we move on, here are some questions to consider:

※ Do you sometimes have unexpected and frightening feelings? Describe.

※ What commitment are you willing to make to stop behaving self-destructively?

※ When you realize you're turning into the Irrational Hulk, how can you deescalate? Take a walk? Go be alone? Pray? Exercise? Call a friend? Write in a journal?

※ Are you clean and sober? If not, what can you do to move in that direction?

※ Does the story of the father and his runaway child ring true for you in any way? How?

Said he very gently in answer to that look, "Don't you know by now that I never think of you as you are now but as you will be when I have brought you to the Kingdom of Love and washed you from all the stains and defilements of the journey?"

It is now time that we look closely at exactly what happened in your abortion experience. Your story needs to be told. By telling it, you can look at it, come to terms with it, and move toward peace and healing.

Let's hear from Rose...

Feeling heard has always been important for my well being, having that connection with other people. It gives me a different perspective and helps me go deeper with things I am struggling with.

Being Heard

What is it about being heard that is so important? We all have a hunger to be heard and acknowledged. It is part of the longing of the human heart that seeks to commune with others. It often seems that everyone is so intent on making themselves heard that they can't just take a little time and give their undivided attention to another. Maybe this is because the default setting of the human heart is selfish and me-centered. It takes energy and discipline to go against the default setting.

These days, to make matters worse, many of us are so glued to our smart devices that we can hardly bear to lift our gaze and meet the eyes of the person in front of us, much less listen to them. When I was younger, people used to make eye contact. That was considered courteous. Now, I find that people don't do that anymore. It might have something to do with the parallax that happens with smart-device cameras—that when you look at the person on the screen of your phone, it looks to them like you're looking down instead of looking at them. If you want the person you're talking to on the phone to have the illusion that you're looking straight at them, you have to look at the tiny camera on the top of the device, not at the screen. It's all terribly awkward and unnatural.

All this adds to a feeling of alienation or being disconnected from others. We don't know how to connect with others anymore. We've become isolated, and, as a result, miss out on some of the sweet rewards of communication, such as learning from other people, finding common ground, and experiencing the affirmation of being heard.

I confess that listening is really hard for me to do. Only because I make a point to practice it quite deliberately am I able to achieve it. I practice listening because I know how bad I am at it, and also because I know how much people need to be heard. One of the ways we can show respect and love is to quiet the voice inside our own head and listen to the other person. Through this book, I want to afford you a space for your story to be heard. I honor your story, even though I may never actually hear it in person. I wish I could sit and listen to all of you because I know you need to be heard. The least I can do for you, as I write and ask you to read what I've written, is to give you the space and encouragement to tell your story. It's my way of showing you respect and love.

There is another who is listening. Think back to the story in the last chapter. Remember the loving father who awaits the return of his rebellious daughter? When that child comes back home, she confesses what she did. She can't hide anything from her dad—he knows her so well. She comes to him repentant and willing to take responsibility. She pours out her heart to her father, and he listens and sees she is broken over her poor choices—and he forgives her. Some of the twists and turns in your story are beyond your control, and other parts of your story fall to you as the responsible party. We all wish we could wiggle out of that uncomfortable position of being to blame, like school children brought before the principal. We know we will have to face consequences and we are afraid. But what if the loving father listening with the greatest interest to your unfolding tale is prepared to accept you back into his arms—to forgive you—if you will only ask him?

Your spiritual father—our way of understanding God—is listening to you too as you proceed with this chapter. He is not listening in order to punish and reject you. He is listening for the inner condition of your heart. Let this telling of your story be your honest confession to him.

A Word about Shame

You might be feeling shame for what occurred. Shame is complicated. At the very least, it is deeply uncomfortable and we want it to go away. At its worst, it can shut us down so we can't move forward toward our goal of peace and healing. Let's unpack shame a bit so we can overcome the danger of becoming immobilized by it. *Merriam-Webster* defines *shame* as "a painful emotion caused by consciousness of guilt, shortcoming, or impropriety." It can come from something we did or from something done to us.

Shame is a fiery motivator. In some cultures, avoiding shame is at the core of family identity. It has everything to do with preserving the honor of a family name. Parents in such cultures might use shame to motivate their children to excel in their studies, or to hold them to a high standard of behavior. "We don't get A minuses in this family!" Applied by caring, committed parents with a healthy measure of encouragement, a child can be strengthened by this application of shame and grow to exceed their own expectations. I was once shamed by a teacher for submitting lousy work. He was sure I could do better. By the end of the term I had discovered my capacity to do excellent work, and that teacher became my favorite, precisely because he didn't allow me to settle for less than the best I could be. Looking at our dictionary definition, this sort of shame would be *consciousness of shortcoming.* We can see that this sort of shame is not necessarily a bad thing.

Shame can also be a very bad thing. It can be a weapon for wounding, used to tear down rather than build up. It can cause irreparable damage in the form of demeaning words or degrading abuses. These wounds of shame twist our sense of who we are. We come to feel we are unworthy of love or consideration. We may become crippled from self-loathing. We may carry these wounds of shame with us our whole lives. Some might even take their lives because their shame is unbearable. Going back to the dictionary definition, this would be *consciousness of impropriety.* Something inappropriate happened to you, and you have to carry that.

You might have been shamed for becoming pregnant. You might have been shamed for getting an abortion. You might have been shamed by your family or your religious community. Or perhaps the shame you feel comes from your own self-assessment. Again, going back to our dictionary definition, shame from your own self-assessment would be *consciousness of guilt.*

In the context of this chapter, in which you will go through the dark valley of revisiting what may be your lowest point in life, I don't bring up shame in order to wound you. Firstly, you have a right to be respected simply as a human being created by God. But more specifically to this context, that you have come this far in the healing process and haven't run away is worthy of respect. Your valiant determination to finish what you've started has earned my highest regard. Hopefully you can acknowledge what you have done and take heart that you are in forward motion, working towards improving a difficult situation.

The shame I wish to speak of is a response to doing wrong. Is there a proper place for shame when we do something wrong? When we know what is right and we do wrong, we naturally feel ashamed. In chapter 1, we talked about right and wrong as God-given ideas. When we look at our actions in the light of God's standards, we all—even the best among us—fall short, and our *consciousness of guilt* is our understanding that we have transgressed those standards. Once God enters the equation in our lives, shame arising from *consciousness of guilt* signals us that what we did was wrong. It should trigger us to run to the forgiving arms of our father, just like the rebellious daughter.

Let's hear from R. Iglesia...

Most of us run from our guilt in the form of frenetic living, anesthetic, even suicide. Freud said blame someone else. But what is the origin of guilt? Guilt is the first symptom of our failing before God. The worse our violation, the worse our sense of guilt and the greater our need. Therefore dealing with guilt must find correction solely on God's terms if we are ever to know relief.

Consciousness of guilt would not be appropriate to the woman who was forced to abort against her will. If she feels shame, her shame is from *consciousness of impropriety.* Her job is *not* to take responsibility for something she had no power to stop, but to grieve the pain of the impropriety perpetrated against her. If this is your story, my heart goes out to you at this moment. Your grief is unique. The question of responsibility may not be so clear cut as one would wish. I have recently heard the story of a woman who was in bondage as a sex slave. She was forced to have abortions, and yet she felt she could have pushed back more forcefully than she did against her handlers. She was trapped in a prisoner's mindset that made clear thinking impossible. As with all who are grappling with this, each of you must discern how much was on you, and where your responsibility ends.

Everyone's story is different, but we all want to come to peace about what happened, and that starts with accepting our part in the story. Once we bravely say what we did and take responsibility for it, then we no longer need the useful signal of shame. We can put it behind us for good.

I am aware that our stories are more complicated than I make them sound here. For many of us, we made the choice, but our reasoning was so twisted that we couldn't properly understand what was taking place. We were operating under misconceptions. So, even while we may have a consciousness of our own guilt, that guilt may be combined with a consciousness of impropriety perpetrated against us by people or even by the culture. It is not my intention to stuff your story into a neat little box. Our stories have a right to be heard on their own terms.

Your Story

So, this chapter is all about your abortion story. It's about what happened, who did what, how you responded, and who is responsible. If you have had multiple abortions, then tell all your stories. Below I have a number of questions for you. Use this book to write in, or get a notebook for your answers if you need more space. Some of the questions won't apply to you. If they don't address your particular situation in a suitable way, or if I haven't asked the right questions, go ahead and use these as a jumping-off point to tell your story in your own way. By writing it down, you own it and can come to terms with it.

These questions may be very hard to answer because of the intense emotions involved. There's no hurry. You may want to take this chapter in small bites and go away and come back. Feel the feelings, and please don't act on your feelings at this time. You may be very raw in the process of digging up these memories. Let's wait until later to contact others you might feel compelled to speak to about their part. Use discretion and thoughtfulness!

Consider the other person. Sometimes it's better to leave people alone and just go through your process without bringing them in. Again, we don't want to compound problems. No blamefests allowed! Let this be your private time for reflecting and feeling. Remember, the goal is to gain an honest appraisal and clear-eyed look at what happened, so you can continue on your path toward peace and healing. Go ahead, I'm listening.

What Happened

✳ How did you get pregnant?

✳ What was going on at the time?

✳ What was your attitude toward being pregnant?

✳ What was your relationship to the father?

✳ Were your parents involved? What was their attitude?

Let's hear from Melissa...

My dad was just furious with me. My mom was more understanding. My parents got married because they had to. Mom got pregnant when she was sixteen years old. Mom convinced Dad that I needed to get an abortion. My mom knew what to do, and she took over. Whatever she told me to do, I would do it. I just thought, If I can get rid of this now, then I won't have to think about it.

❀ Who encouraged the abortion? Who discouraged it?

❀ Whose final decision was it?

❀ Were there cultural influences that led to the decision?

❀ Was there discussion beforehand?

❀ What was the father's attitude toward the abortion?

❀ What were your priorities at the time?

❀ Were you coerced, pressured, lied to, threatened, or mistreated in the process?

❀ Did you lie or in any way hurt or mistreat others in the process (I mean besides the baby)?

Immediate Effects

☀ How were you treated by the practitioners at the clinic?

☀ Did you experience pain?

☀ Were there complications?

☀ Have you experienced consequences in your body as a result of the abortion (e.g., miscarriage, uterine scarring, pain, infertility, etc.)?

Let's hear from Melissa...

For my second pregnancy when I was carrying my daughter, I had an "incompetent cervix," I think a direct result of my abortion, where the cervix wants to open up prematurely. Early on in the pregnancy I was 3 cm dilated and 80 percent effaced and I had to go on bed rest immediately.

Aftermath

❊ How did your relationship with the father of the child change?

❊ Were other relationships affected?

❊ What have you gone through since then?

❊ How has your view of the experience changed since it took place?

Let's hear from Tammy...

I had multiple miscarriages after my abortion. By that time my husband and I really wanted kids, so this was very devastating. One of them happened at home. I went to the doctor and took with me what had come out. I'll never forget on the written report for the lab analysis, they called it "non-specific tissue." That just felt so impersonal. That was my baby.

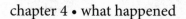

Our Children

Our culture has done a very efficient job of dehumanizing the child in the womb. Let's hear from a former abortionist about the moment her eyes were opened to realize that, by providing abortions, she was participating in the killing of children. She is speaking about a time when a good friend of hers asked her to read an article comparing abortion to the Nazi Holocaust of World War II:

> My dad was in World War II, and he was there when the first concentration camp was liberated. So I grew up with all those pictures and stories, and when I became a doctor, I couldn't understand how the German doctors could do what they did. And so, as I read that article, I suddenly realized how they could do what they did, because they were just like me. They didn't consider the fetus as a human being.[1]

Listen to these words from the Hebrew Bible. The psalmist expresses the Creator's intimate knowledge of his creation, even in the womb:

> For you formed my inward parts; You wove me in my mother's womb. I will give thanks to You, for I am fearfully and wonderfully made; Wonderful are Your works, and my soul knows it very well. My frame was not hidden from You, when I was made in secret, and skillfully wrought in the depths of the earth; Your eyes have seen my unformed substance; and in Your book were all written the days that were ordained for me, when as yet there was not one of them.[2]

Very likely, you have had your own moment of realization that your abortion took the life of your child. This may be the most difficult part of coming to grips with abortion, because it brings

---

1. "From Abortionist to Pro-Life Advocate: A Story of God's Redemption, Part 1 - Dr. Kathi Aultman," YouTube interview from *Focus on the Family* (January 22, 2020), focusonthefamily.com/pro-life/kathi-aultman-why-i-am-no-longer-an-abortionist/.
2. Psalm 139:13–16.

us face to face with harm we caused—not to ourselves—but to an innocent child.

※ What was your view, prior to the abortion, of the one living inside of you?

※ How did that view change after the abortion?

※ Are you able to say that you are the parent of that child?

Prepare a Room

This is a lot to deal with. Can I suggest, as one who cares about you, that you take a pause right now before we go on with this chapter? Put down the book, go, and do something else for awhile. Take a walk. Chill. Come back later with a refreshed outlook.

Hopefully, you took a breather, and now you're ready to continue.

A Word about Responsibility

We have an opportunity to get some clarity about who was responsible for what. Moving forward with healing cannot take place if we're either blaming others for what is our part while ducking and hiding from responsibility ourselves, or blaming ourselves for what is not our part.

We can look at our stories from the point of view of being in the midst of the trees, or we can get some altitude and see the forest—the bigger picture. You will need to learn to dance between the forest view and the trees view. There is value in a subjective telling of your story, and value in a more objective telling. The subjective telling gives you the satisfaction of a deeply personal and emotional catharsis—saying it all and feeling all the feelings. The value of the objective telling comes from being able to make evaluations of what occurred without the sometimes-distorted, intensely subjective vantage point. Stepping back allows you some perspective, to untangle the threads and see clearly who did what and why. It brings out compassion—for others as well as for yourself. You can see motives more clearly. For example, "My boyfriend gave me the money and drove me to the clinic. I have resented him for that, but looking more objectively, I can see that he didn't know any better than I did just what we were doing." You want to see things as they truly are and let your emotions be appropriate to match the facts of the case. In either case, what matters most is the truth.

What does it mean to take responsibility? It means being brave to face the truth about the part you played. It means confessing it and acting responsibly from this moment onward. Do as Anna sings in the Disney movie *Frozen II*. In her time of grief and confusion, Anna can't see the path before her, so she determines to "just do the next right thing." Precisely how one acts is unique in each case, but, at the very least, you might start by speaking the following aloud: "This is what I did. This is what happened because of what I did. This is who got hurt. This is how I feel about it now."

You can say these words to yourself alone, or, if you're part of a group, you might share with the group or an individual in the group. If you're not in a group, can you identify a trusted friend who can be a confidante? Speaking the words aloud to someone allows for you to more fully take responsibility by owning up, or "taking ownership," as they say. If you have no one to confide in, continue writing in your book. In any case, please also consider letting God—your loving father—hear your story from your lips as well.

Taking responsibility might mean you need to go further and ask yourself, How can I make amends without causing more hurt? Think about it carefully. Now is not the time to act. We'll discuss in chapter 10 how to take action. All your actions should come from thoughtful reflection, not from the passion of this raw, emotional moment.

☀ For what part of the abortion are others responsible?

☀ For what part of it are you responsible?

☀ Have you taken responsibility?

☀ Are you blaming others for things for which you need to take responsibility?

Let's hear from Katie...

Even though I assigned some blame to the doctor for bad or incomplete information, the onus was mine. My need for being loved overweighed my good sense. It took another 12–15 years to get back on a track of some life responsibility.

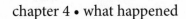

A Word about Forgiveness

Taking responsibility is a tough pill to swallow. To make the process sweeter, we apply compassion—we want to receive it, and we offer it to others. As we look back at that person we used to be when we made those poor choices, compassion toward ourselves eases the pain of having done wrong. Zoom out to that forest view we talked about and look at the whole story with loving eyes. Be a friend to that hurting person that was you going through an awful time.

Likewise, as we look back at others who hurt us along the way, finding compassion for them allows us to let go of the hurt (Here comes another Disney *Frozen* song—"Let it go, let it go..." I'm an animator—I can't help myself!). Unforgiveness clings to the hurt, while forgiveness releases it and frees us from resentment and bitterness, which only damage us, not the other person.

Remember the loving father in our story of the rebellious daughter. When she came to him contrite and honest and confessing, he forgave her, and from that moment forward, she was embraced back into her family and restored to an inheritance that surpassed her wildest dreams. Now just imagine how that child would be so eager to forgive others after receiving such a huge gift of forgiveness from her father. That can be your story too. Be eager to forgive.

❀ Are there people from whom you need to ask forgiveness?

❀ Are there people you need to forgive?

❀ If you were to ask God, the loving father, to forgive you, would you be able to receive and accept his forgiveness?

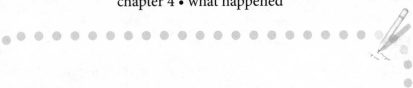

Lament

I suspect that this process of detailing your abortion experience has stirred up deep sorrow for many of you. Please remember that there is a proper time for weeping and mourning. You have heard it said that, "To everything there is a season, and a time to every purpose under the heaven.... A time to weep, and a time to laugh; a time to mourn, and a time to dance."[3] If this is that time of weeping and mourning for you, honor that by not running away from it. Take the time to grieve.

Let's hear from Esther-Ruth...

Culturally speaking, my community is not all that keen on counseling, therapy, and all that kind of stuff. The idea that "I can power my way through it" is really big. So we're more likely to push it down and keep moving rather than dealing with emotions. It's the shame and the guilt. We women have always had to be strong and do what we need to do for our families and to survive. There was really no time for emotions or processing or talking about feelings. I think that needs to shift a lot.

We may be tempted to push down our feelings and "power our way through it," as Esther-Ruth says. But lament is part of the healing process. For some of you, just allowing yourself to weep and mourn is nearly impossible. Yet it is an appropriate response to all you've been through. One author writing on lament tells us:

Finding an explanation or a quick solution for grief, while an admirable goal, can circumvent the opportunity afforded in lament—to give a person permission to wrestle with sorrow instead of rushing to end it. Walking through sorrow without understanding and embracing the God-given song of lament can stunt the grieving process.[4]

---

3. Ecclesiastes 3:1, 4.
4. Mark Vroegop, *Dark Clouds, Deep Mercy: Discovering the Grace of Lament* (Wheaton, IL: Crossway, 2019).

God is fluent in the wordless language of lament. We were not meant to carry the weight of our sorrow alone. Here is a description of the promised Messiah of God, whom the prophet Isaiah foretold. This Messiah has the power and strength to bear our griefs:

> He was despised and forsaken of men, a man of sorrows and acquainted with grief.... Surely our griefs He Himself bore, and our sorrows He carried.[5]

It's so hard to be a human being! As I think about how our decisions resound through our lives and touch the lives of others, sometimes with tragic, irreversible consequences, I have to weep too. I am lamenting with you. We are so broken as a species. We suffer so much hurting. What can possibly relieve the pain? What is the effective medicine for our human ailment?

I have some ideas about how those questions might be answered. We will discuss that next.

For now, I hope you won't mind if I return once again to Disney's *Frozen II*. The words to this song from that animated film touch me so deeply at this moment, that I must share them with you. Maybe we can have a good cry together.[6]

> *Where the north wind meets the sea,*
> *there's a mother full of memory.*
> *Come, my darling, homeward bound.*
> *Where all is lost, then all is found.*
> *All is found.*
> *All is found.*

---

5. Isaiah 53:3–4.
6. Kristen Anderson-Lopez and Robert Lopez, "All Is Found," 2019, from *Frozen II*, Wonderland Music Company, Walt Disney. I love the Kacey Musgraves version.

Prepare a Room

5 what is love?

"The High Places," answered the Shepherd, "are the starting places for the journey down to the lowest place in the world. When you have hinds' feet and can go 'leaping on the mountains and skipping on the hills,' you will be able, as I am, to run down from the heights in gladdest self-giving and then go up to the mountains again. You will be able to mount to the High Places swifter than eagles, for it is only up on the High Places of Love that anyone can receive the power to pour themselves down in an utter abandonment of self-giving."

*L*ove. It is the favorite go-to word, tossed about almost as a verbal tic. It can be used for every kind of idea in every kind of context. I love sushi. I love my pillow. I love finding a bargain. I love seeing the speedster on the highway get stopped by the Highway Patrol. In just these few examples we see food taste preference, the human need to be comfortable during sleep, an imperative to be thrifty, and a sense of fairness that needs to see justice done. My husband loves to work with wood. He loves politics.

He loves that I keep the house clean. In just those few examples we see love of nature, the need to stay informed to survive in a complicated world, and appreciation of the benefits of marriage.

While versatile enough to carry these many shades of meaning and more, the word *love* also carries weightier ideas about committed, lifelong relationships found in families, friendships, and marriages. One deeper meaning of the word *love* is particularly relevant to our healing process. We will call it *greatest love*, and we will explore how it will provide a firm foundation on which you can build a wholesome and fulfilling future.

In the last chapter you bravely wrote your story. In this chapter, nestled at the very heart of our journey, we will open a door to a new stage of your story. In *greatest love*, we find the key that has potential to make all the difference in our healing process. We will discover how mistaken ideas about love steer us away from fulfillment, and how the real medicine of *greatest love* can heal what ails us.

The Quality of Love

We all want to be loved, and we have a yearning for affirmation. We are not islands, so we reach for the company of others to fill that yearning. We enter into relationships with the desire that they will last, and we hurt when they are broken. We seek trustworthy friends and perhaps a life partner as husband or wife. We build families, and our relationships expand. Yet, in trying to love and be loved, we can often feel like travelers in a strange land where we don't speak the language. Love can sometimes be foreign and inscrutable.

We may think we are experiencing love when we have a warm feeling well up inside us, or when we are swept up in the momentary rush of being "in love," or when we give our bodies to another in sexual union. Those are not necessarily indications of greatest love, but rather, often they indicate feelings aroused by our great need *to be loved*. This hunger to be seen, heard, and acknowledged by others makes us more focused on ourselves than on the other person. This can leave us unsatisfied.

Loving others is not easy, as demonstrated by how often marriages collapse, friendships break down, and family members become alienated. As a mother, wife, parent, daughter, student, teacher, friend, sister, and grandmother, I have spent a lifetime grasping for love and missing it entirely. This has given me the opportunity to learn the hard way over and over how the counterfeit falls short of the real thing. I began my experience of love like a starving person fighting everyone around me over a scrap of bread. I was starving for attention, for affirmation, for something to soothe my unease. I couldn't afford giving too much, for fear my own needs wouldn't be met. My needs were always foremost in my mind. These unfortunate qualities in me got in the way of love. I thought I was practicing love, but my knowledge of it was limited. How could I know what I didn't know?

The good news for me is that I encountered a new way of understanding love—what we are calling *greatest love*. It completely changed me and has affected all my relationships. Against all odds, my marriage survived. It became the crucible in which I slowly and gradually began to practice this new understanding and to learn what love really is. After putting my new understanding into practice, my marriage and other relationships grew beyond my wildest hopes. This did not come easily or naturally—it was not my default setting—yet I persisted in practicing and saw results, in spite of my handicaps. This chapter comes out of what I have learned about what love is and what it isn't.

Let's start by looking at an epidemic afflicting women today that particularly undermines love.

"You Go, Girl!"

I wonder how many of you have been raised in the "You go, Girl!" culture. I was bombarded from a young age with a message I heard from my parents, and later in schools and, even more, in the culture of movies, literature, and music. That message was, "You go,

Girl!" and it meant that I was not to be constrained by limitations put on me by anyone or any circumstance. Being female was not an obstacle to realizing any dreams I dared to dream. The more ambitious the dream, the more the applause I received from family and teachers. I could have it all. I was encouraged to aspire in a career, be a strong woman, pursue my passions, "follow my bliss," change the world, grab the brass ring, break the glass ceiling.

Quite an ambitious set of expectations for such a fairly ordinary young lady as myself. In the back of my mind I couldn't help but wonder where motherhood fit in such grandiose visions of accomplishment. Most of us women, after all, do end up wanting to have families some time in our lives. How do diapers fit in with bliss and the glass ceilings we're supposed to be breaking on our way to the top? Looking back, it all seems like a recipe for disappointment. So much potential exploding on my imagination couldn't help but suffer road rash once it encountered the real world.

The word *deserve* figured prominently in the message that screamed at me along the way, like, "I deserve to do what I want!" "I deserve to be loved!" "I deserve to pursue my dreams without being held back by having a child."

Things in the culture have not changed since I grew up. In fact, the only change is that this message to girls has become louder, more insistent, and more extreme. Young ladies these days often suffer from entitlement mentality, an attitude based on the notion that they are deserving of special privileges that others don't deserve. While we all deserve basic human rights and respect—life, liberty, and the pursuit of happiness, you might say—we are not entitled to special privileges beyond what is common to all people.

From an online mag that describes its purpose as inspiring single women "to lead fulfilling lives as single women (because a partner is NOT a requirement for an amazing life)," comes a recent article entitled, "Why Are So Many Smart, Gorgeous Women Single? It's Almost an Epidemic." Responding to the question it poses: "We're smart, funny and basically total catches...so where are all the great guys?" here are some answers given:

Since we know our worth, *we won't accept anything less than what we deserve from guys.* They need to be on our level in every sense of the word and if they're not prepared to do that, we're not prepared to date them.... We've got busy careers, amazing friends, loving families, and passions to pursue. Our schedules are booked solid.[1]

This way of understanding relationships may seem woman-affirming, but it actually handicaps the pursuit of love. What do we get from an entitlement attitude, and what is the price paid for its rewards? You may have noticed that women these days tend to be domineering, aggressive, and self-centered. So, maybe what these bold lasses get is they move higher up on the corporate ladder, or they get their way, or they never have to hold their tongues, or they get to be alpha next to a submissive beta-man.

But is this smart, gorgeous, single woman ever going to discover the fulfillment of a true experience of love? Her attitude will repulse love rather than cultivating it. In fact, entitlement is incompatible with successful relationships, because love has been sacrificed on the altar of self-promotion. The "You go, Girl!" culture is not about love. Teach a young woman to be entitled, and you will set her up for a future of loneliness and nonfulfillment.

Some of these women are starting to get to the stage of their lives when they are seeing the fruits of this attitude. Here's writer Aimée Lutkin in an article discussing her single life:

Anchoring my existence without the signposts of commitment, or children, is a lot of work, and sometimes I feel myself giving up on it, drifting off into a grey directionless space in danger of floating completely away.[2]

The "You go, Girl!" guiding principle points women in the exact opposite direction from love that is fulfilling. So many have been

1. Jennifer Still, "Why Are So Many Smart, Gorgeous Women Single? It's Almost an Epidemic," *Bolde*, bolde.com, emphasis mine.
2. Aimée Lutkin, "When Can I Say I'll Be Alone Forever?" *Jezebel*, December 25, 2016, jezebel.com.

influenced—not only in their abortion experiences, but in all their relationships—by this deeply selfish impulse. It has been tried and found wanting. In short, it's not good for women. They long for something that feeds them, and "You go, Girl!" feeds them only more of themselves, until the taste of "me" and "more me" has gone stale in their mouths. Girls have been led down a fruitless path under the assumption that their worth comes from their efforts to puff themselves up with empty affirmation. Along that path they have made decisions—including their abortions—that have turned life sour.

It's not that girls shouldn't have dreams and pursue their goals—they should indeed develop their gifts and seek after excellence in all they do. They have much to offer to benefit the world. Their successes are to be applauded. The problem comes when they are encouraged to pursue their dreams without core principles that give meaning to their lives.

Once these women arrive at a certain age, a cognitive dissonance occurs in the collision between the message of the culture and the message from the maternal urges of their own bodies. This dissonance can be found at the root of many psychological maladies. Only by acknowledging the shortcomings of the self-centered life, turning around 180 degrees, and traveling in the opposite direction can they finally discover the real, restorative love that does give meaning to life.

Why is the "You go, Girl!" culture relevant to a chapter on love? Why spend so much time looking at this phenomenon? Aren't there plenty of examples besides this one of people in the culture today missing the boat on love? Yes, there may be. But I see this particular problem as likely responsible for a lot of abortions and for a lot of wounded women. At its worst, it results in destructive behaviors, as girls fill their cravings for self-affirmation with binge eating, reckless drug and alcohol use, sexual promiscuity, and other pitfalls that tear them down and ruin their lives. In recognizing its destructive influence, we lay bare the shortcomings of this way of life and begin to overcome the damage done.

Greatest Love

Let's turn now to the remedy. The teaching on greatest love came from what for me was an unexpected source. I am Jewish, and as a Jew, I never imagined there might be something to be gained from looking at one who is largely dismissed by my people, even though he is also a Jew. I refer to the first-century rabbi named Jesus. Yet, this seeming stranger seized my attention with words that challenged my self-centered thinking and changed me forever. In spite of initial resistance rising from cultural and religious objections, this Jesus pierced my heart with a new understanding of the Hebrew Bible. This is because he is the fulfillment of those ancient Scriptures.

> God, after He spoke long ago to the fathers in the prophets in many portions and in many ways, in these last days has spoken to us in His Son, whom He appointed heir of all things, through whom also He made the world. And He is the radiance of His glory and the exact representation of His nature, and upholds all things by the word of His power.[3]

In the Torah, or the first five books of Moses, and in the prophets and the psalms, this Son of God is predicted as one who will be a child born, a Son given, while also being "Mighty God, Eternal Father, and Prince of Peace."[4] Because he is God and also a human being who suffered, we can look to him as our hope in the midst of our suffering humanity. Let's look at how his teachings on love can bring us to a new place.

When we look to Jesus for his teachings on love, we find them rooted in the Torah. Leviticus 19:18 tells us to "love your neighbor as yourself," and Jesus makes this seemingly incidental command—easily missed among over six hundred other laws in the Torah—the centerpiece of his teachings. He even distinguishes it by labeling it "my commandment."

---

3. Hebrews 1:1–3.
4. Isaiah 9:6.

During Jesus's last Passover Seder,[5] commonly called the Last Supper, he presents a very powerful teaching about love. Quite simply, he says that "no one has greater love than this—that one lays down his life for his friends."[6] That is, he is boldly defining the greatest form of love—just as you might say, for example, that Handel's Messiah is the highest form of music, or the Lamborghini is auto design taken to its apex. These are the best of the best, la crème de la crème, the cream of the crop, the pinnacle, the zenith. The highest height of love, Jesus says, is when we go low—when we put aside our life for the sake of someone else—when we take our focus off ourselves and allow it to settle on another. Just as we would do with a huge vase of flowers blocking the view of the people around the dinner table, we are to set ourselves over to the side so we can have a fresh view of others. Once we can see them, we are to serve them. We are to consider their needs above our own. We are to act not for our own best interests, but for the best interests of the other person.

Instead of asserting authority over his followers, Jesus surprises everyone by his willingness to be a servant. During that Passover Seder—a ritual that features a lot of hand washing—he ties a towel around his waist, gets on his knees, and washes his followers' feet. And those feet are not powdered with Dr. Scholl's odor remover—they are feet that wear the same sandals every day and tread dirty streets. He does this as an example of how we are to treat one another.

In case there is some question about what it means to love one another, Jesus explains exactly how we are to do so: "*Just as I have loved you*, you also are to love one another."[7] So we are to use his example of loving as our model. How does he love others? His love fulfills that definition he gives of greatest love, which is to lay down his life for his friends. This he does by willingly giving

---

5. A Seder is a Jewish ritual meal commemorating the deliverance of the Jews from slavery in Egypt.
6. John 15:13 NET.
7. John 13:34 NET, emphasis added.

his life to serve rather than be served. By humbling himself in this way, he shows us the sweetness of self-sacrificial love.

We even see this self-sacrificial love reflected in our story of the father and his rebellious daughter. Remember that the father extends himself to embrace his returning daughter before he even knows why she's coming up the path.[8] She may be about to reject him again, yet he's able to lay his pride and his dignity aside to extend himself in love. When we look at how this represents the love father God has for us, that gives our lives value, we see that God loves us so much that he is willing to suffer indignity just to bring us into his embrace.

Left to our own devices, we will choose the selfish path. Jesus inspires us to overcome our limitations by his example. His ideal of love is counterintuitive to all urges we have as human beings. Diligence is required to learn it. Learning greatest love takes a commitment to hard work over the long-term. We can start to cultivate it by becoming aware of it. From there, we set ourselves goals and—as I like to tell you—take small bites.

Pennies in the Bank of Love

By way of example, I began to put this teaching on love into practice with a simple task in my marriage. If my husband asked me to do something, like get him some coffee, the first thing that would happen is a voice in my head would say, "What am I, your maid? Get your own d*** coffee!" But, instead of acting on that, I would put down whatever I was doing and quickly go get him the coffee. I had to move quickly because I didn't want to give my selfish default setting an opportunity to kick in.

What would have been the result if I had acted on my initial impulse? My husband would have been wounded and felt un-cared for. He would have begun to wonder what sort of partner I was, that I couldn't be counted on to consider his needs. Trust between us would have suffered a blow. On my end, I would have

---

8. Hat tip to Jill Carattini, "Telling Stories," *A Slice of Infinity*, February 9, 2020.

been righteously indignant at being asked to serve him. My pride would have gotten puffed all out of proportion at his expense. We would have been at cross purposes, and it would have taken time to heal. Add up a few dozen or more of those over the course of a year of marriage and see where you end up.

What was the result when, instead, I got him the coffee he asked for? I was not greatly inconvenienced by it, I assure you. My husband was appreciative and eager to do nice things for me in return, and we went on our ways with smiles on our faces. In addition to that, I had the satisfaction of knowing I had done something nice for the man I love. Don't we want to make our loved ones happy? Making him happy makes me happy, and my husband wants the same for me. A common compliment I hear from my husband when I cook him a meal is, "I can taste the love." That's because—whatever the task is we choose to do for the other, whether fetching coffee, cleaning the toilet, making eggs, or washing the car—it's not the thing you're doing that's important, but the message of love and caring that's contained in the doing.

When I started this practice, I couldn't help but begin to notice other couples that clung to the idea that "fetching this for my husband" or "helping my wife with that" somehow threatened their dignity. I was particularly sensitive to these situations because they so closely resembled me before I started my new practice of greatest love. These people suddenly seemed terribly petty from my new perspective. They preserve their pride, but at what cost? Who likes to be around the person who considers herself too good to do small things for others?

My little practice made it possible for me to love sacrificially when a bigger issue came before us. My husband had a dream of building a house, which we pursued despite my reluctance. Fulfilling my husband's dream required that we live in very crude circumstances during more than five years of construction. That was the last thing I wanted to do. I enjoyed my comfortable home, having a washing machine and a flush toilet and doors and a warm place to lay my head at night. I had to give up all that and other comforts in this new scheme of his.

But because I honored my husband's vision, I laid my life aside as an expression of love for him and willingly went along. Our new life was not easy, but by then I had become more practiced at loving sacrificially, so I was able to be gracious (mostly!) through a very challenging time. I didn't behave perfectly—sometimes I just couldn't stand the grinding sounds of circular saws and earth compactors, and not having bathroom walls—that was really tough. But all in all, guided by Jesus's concept of greatest love, my husband and I remained harmonious through the difficult building process.

My husband has a way of looking at the sacrifices husbands and wives make for each other. He likes to say that when you love sacrificially, you are "putting pennies in the bank of love." Well, I guess I had a lot of pennies in my bank account from the house-building project, because later, when I needed to recover from surgery, I found in my husband the most doting, caring, and attentive caregiver imaginable. He helped me in my recovery with the same sacrificial love I had given him in the pursuit of his house-building dream. By now in our marriage, we are completely satisfied that we are loved by one other and getting the very best of what the other has to give. The quality of love we give and receive as husband and wife is a big part of our sense of fulfilling our life's purpose, and we radiate that love throughout our family and community of friends.

I like the way this rabbi, who writes on the problem of loneliness in marriage, spoke in a recent interview:

> The focus on *what I'm getting* from the marriage can often get in the way. It's not what I get, it's what I contribute.... When you don't want to improve yourself anymore, you are ready to invite someone else into your life, and you can focus on the other. That's why, if you're married for some *thing*, every *thing* is really for you. Whereas—the other person—you're there for

them. So I think if you just don't worry about what you're getting from the marriage, and focus on what you're giving, [your marriage] will deepen and will become more intimate.[9]

I assure you, I need to be reminded to practice greatest love on a daily basis. Going to that offended place, where you get the sickly sweet reward of self-pity and indignation, comes most naturally to me. A needy, insecure child inside me still worries, "What if I give and don't get back?" But here lies the supernatural math of greatest love: Two plus two no longer equals four in this love equation—two plus two equals a million. When we give love self-sacrificially, we don't get back in kind, we get back something exponentially above and beyond what we give. It may seem that getting the focus off yourself will deprive you of the attention you need, but the truth is just the opposite. The deep well of love that opens before you when you lay aside your life for others feeds you as well, and the lover becomes the beloved, as in my own personal examples above. When Jesus made this claim about greatest love, he had in mind the exquisite reward that comes from acting *against* our natural human tendencies.

The theme of self-sacrificial love shows up in movies and books, and when it does, we can't help but be moved in a way that other themes can't approach. It resonates with us because it is an exalted expression not native to human beings. Rather, it demonstrates the best of what human beings can be when they transcend themselves. Self-sacrifice is what heroes do.

You already know that I am an animator. I love to see movies, and animation in particular. I think of the Disney/Pixar animation *Inside Out*, in which a girl named Riley is guided by emotions that act out within a "control center" inside her mind. Remember Riley's imaginary friend Bing Bong that looks like a sort of elephant creature? He sacrifices his life so that the character Joy can escape the pit of forgetfulness and go on to help Riley. In the

---

9. Rabbi Manis Friedman (author of *The Joy of Intimacy*), "Intimacy vs. Loneliness," *The Dennis Prager Show*, January 22, 2020, emphasis added.

movie *Titanic*, we see Jack sacrifice his life so Rose can live. In the 1998 film *The Thin Red Line*, one soldier deliberately places himself in danger and gives his life to distract the enemy so that those in his company can be saved. The father Lee sacrifices his life to save his children in *A Quiet Place*. I'm sure you can think of many more examples from your own viewing and reading. These are moments that highlight the most beautiful of human qualities, precisely because it is so far above what is natural to us.

Greatest Love in Action

Where do we see self-sacrificial love in practice in the real world? We see it dramatically acted out in the daily work of first responders—the ones who run into the burning building instead of away from it—those who risk their own safety to rescue others. We see it in the soldiers willing to give their lives for the sake of their nation, in the caregivers who risk their own health to serve those with deadly illnesses—doctors in hazmat suits treating coronavirus patients. We see it in adult children caring for their aging parents in their final days. Strangers buying Thanksgiving dinner for the needy, or neighbors making meals for new parents, or acquaintances taking fire victims into their homes, or someone paying for the groceries of the person behind them in line. In a million little ways each and every day we participate in selfless acts of giving, sometimes as the recipients and sometimes as the givers. Even that difficult task of listening is a form of this greatest love, as we put aside our need to be in the spotlight to give the other person the satisfaction of being heard.

I find an irony in this greatest love, in that we are to offer it self-sacrificially without regard for personal gain, yet self-sacrifice turns out to have wonderful rewards. The one who loves in this way is blessed firstly with a gentle assurance that comes from doing a good turn. What is more, self-sacrificial giving grows us up by building our discipline. We don't have to be ruled any longer by our voracious hunger to have our way and be the center of attention. We develop self-control, moderation, and a lean appetite.

Self-indulgence becomes distasteful as we learn to delay or even cancel gratification. We are no longer demanding children, but thoughtful adults. Additionally, we open ourselves up to that experience of love that is exquisite, ineffable, and out of proportion to what we give. Perhaps the greatest reward of all is that the other person receives love. Their needs are filled. These are great incidental rewards for doing something without seeking reward!

Think of how your heart has been humbled and touched with gratitude on those occasions when someone has set their needs aside for you. Think of how you have received the gift of peace when you have set your needs aside for another. This is the foundation on which successful relationships are built. The husband and wife who consider the other's needs before their own are on the road to developing trust that can last a lifetime. They care for one another during life's storms, they watch one another's backs, and they share the pleasures and joys of the good times. Working for the well being of the other makes them a unified team. That is what marriage is supposed to be.

One place we often see greatest love in practice is in parenting. Mothers and fathers lay aside their lives so that their children can live well. Children may not have an awareness of what has been set aside for their sake, yet the self-sacrificial parents set themselves aside anyway, without thought of personal gain. Instead of pursuing her art career, Mom changes poopy diapers and develops art projects for her kids to do. Instead of staying in that carefree lifestyle, Dad commits to getting up at 4 a.m. daily for his commute to the job that will keep his family afloat.

Let's hear from Katie...

Being a woman is a balancing act, meant for the strong. We are required to support and care for others and not ask too much in return.

As children grow and mature, they begin to practice the self-sacrificial love they are witnessing in their parents by letting little brother go first, or giving the last bite of cake to Grandpa, or cleaning up the spill even though sister caused it.

Let's be sure we understand that setting yourself aside for another is not the same as being a doormat. If you are being taken advantage of in a relationship, that is not healthy. There is no excuse for abuse of any sort, and appropriate action should be taken if you find yourself on the receiving end of someone's verbal, physical, sexual, financial, or emotional abuse. Sacrificial giving must at all times be *your choice*, not something forced on you. Love given under compulsion is not love at all. Freedom to love or not love is precisely what gives our love weight—because we could have chosen not to love, but instead we choose to love—we *freely* lay ourselves aside for another. Giving sacrificially should be uplifting for both parties, as a reflection of Jesus's highest hopes for humanity. It should not be demeaning. If you are having a hard time making this distinction, please seek wise counsel from someone outside your situation that you can trust to guide you into the proper steps to take.

"Go low, Girl!"

Where is your fulfillment found? I believe that if you are seeking fulfillment in self-promotion before all else, you will end up empty. Fulfillment is found in the practice of this greatest love that Jesus described. When you make room for others and give of yourself with kindness, patience, peacemaking, and gentleness, you are fulfilled in a way you never could be by pursuing self-centered goals, because you have used your life to make someone else's life better. The practice of self-sacrificial love will lead to greater success in all your relationships, and set you up for lifelong marriage satisfaction. When you go with the best and highest form of love, you bring out the best in others. This greatest love has the power to transform strife and enmity in relationships into reconciliation and peace. It can have dramatic restorative effect.

Now let's bring this new understanding back to the subject of abortion. As we begin to piece together our lives after abortion, an understanding of greatest love as taught by Jesus becomes a key tool for rebuilding. As we reflect on our abortion experience, it is clear to see that we did not exercise greatest love with our unborn children. For most of us, the decision to abort was made from selfish motives. In fact, our children were the ones that were unwittingly sacrificed for our sake. That is the exact opposite of how the parent-child relationship ought to be. Jesus's picture of greatest love teaches us what our relationship with those children could have been. The way we parented our children lost in abortion has devastated us. But that does not have to be the end of the story. Once we are able to see how our faulty notions of love have led us in the wrong direction, we can turn around and start pursuing the real, nourishing love that has the power to set all our relationships back on solid ground. This laying aside of our lives for others is the foundation on which a future of peace and healing is built. Once you are set on the right path to love with greatest love, you will be able to shed the guilt, shame, and self-condemnation for how your love fell short in the past. Now that you have a different vision of what love can be, you can start sacrificially loving all your loved ones, including your lost children. We will develop this idea further later, when you prepare a room for your child lost in abortion.

Instead of the "You go, Girl!" approach to living, how about a new slogan for a new way of life: "Go low, Girl!" Others can be on top, indulge their every whim, puff themselves up, be right all the time, get huffy when someone offends them, and insist on stuff they think they deserve. You and I are on a different path, one that achieves the highest heights by going low.

❋ How do you think putting into practice the teaching on greatest love might affect your relationships?

❋ What is a small step you can take to develop your practice of greatest love?

❋ What would it mean for you to become a "Go low, Girl"?

Prepare a Room

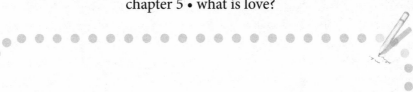

6 mother-hood

Look not upon me with contempt,
Though soiled and marred I be,
The King found me—an outcast thing—
And set his love on me.
I shall be perfected by Love,
Made fair as day to see.

The design of the human body is awe inspiring and miraculous. In our bodies, a synchronized symphony of operations performs in perfect harmony to sustain us and further our species. Without thinking about it, we breathe in and out some twenty times per minute. Our lungs extract oxygen from the air we breathe, and our hearts pump red blood cells carrying that oxygen and other nutrients to the ten trillion cells in our bodies. Human cells are self-contained, living entities that move around, communicate, replicate, and utilize energy for specific purposes. Our cells help us exchange oxygen for carbon dioxide, secrete digestive juices to extract nutrients from our lunch, and expel irritants from our lungs by coughing. The neurons in our nervous systems send electrical signals that enable us to dance, feel pain, and solve problems.[1] All these and innumerable other operations, involving eleven distinct and complex systems, occur in our bodies involuntarily. We inhabit a fantastic, well-oiled machine not of our making. One can't help but conclude that this beautiful design has been put in place with a specific purpose in mind: that of reflecting God's love.

> When I look up at the heavens, which your fingers made, and see the moon and the stars, which you set in place, of what importance is the human race, that you should notice them? Of what importance is mankind, that you should pay attention to them, and make them a little less than the heavenly beings? You grant mankind honor and majesty.[2]

Birds and Bees and Babies

Let's take a peek at some of the amazing automatic operations that occur during reproduction. All the eggs a woman will ever have in her ovaries throughout her lifetime are fully present by the time she is a twenty-week-old fetus in the womb. She starts out with six to seven million eggs. Gradually, over the course of her life in utero and as she is born and lives, most of them become absorbed as nutrition for the other eggs.[3]

During her monthly cycle, the texture of a woman's fluids changes. In the fertile part of her cycle, her fluids become more mucous, giving the sperm the perfect highway to reach the egg. Sperm and egg come together against all odds deep within the woman's fallopian tubes. After fertilization, the egg is nudged toward the womb, even as its cells are multiplying at a terrific

1. Rob Houston, sr. ed., *How the Body Works* (New York: Dorling Kindersley Ltd./Penguin Random House, 2016), 12–15, 112–121.
2. Psalm 8:3–5 NET.
3. James W. Wood, *Dynamics of Human Reproduction* (New Brunswick: Aldine-Transaction, 2009), 122.

rate. The woman's hormones go to work immediately to promote implantation of the fertilized egg in the womb wall and to develop nourishment for the growing child.

The placenta is a nutrition factory that shares the womb with the baby and delivers oxygen and blood from mother to baby through the umbilical cord. Progesterone and other hormones are secreted from the placenta, supporting and maintaining a healthy "womb room" for the growing child and preparing Mom's breasts to eventually feed the baby.

In preparation for birth, another hormone causes the woman's joints to loosen up in order to accommodate the fully developed baby that will pass through her pelvis at the birth. The woman's cervix, securely closed during pregnancy to protect the baby, also prepares for birth by softening, thinning, and opening. Uterine muscles begin to contract so that the baby is pushed out. In navigating the birth canal, the baby automatically twists and rotates so that its shoulders—its widest point—can pass through the narrow pelvic opening.

...and Breasts and Bonds

Meanwhile, during the pregnancy, the mother's breasts have been preparing to sustain the baby that is to emerge. They become fuller, as they develop the capacity to produce milk. The dark areas around the nipple, the areolae, grow dark in color, so that the newborn with its blurry eyesight can find the target. The mother is a highly efficient feeding factory, on top of everything else.

My favorite of all the awesome phenomena in the perfect design of baby and mother is a wonderful baby dance called the *breast crawl*. Within minutes of birth, if the newborn is placed on the mom's abdomen, he or she will slowly and gradually push in a stepping motion up toward the mother's breasts, unaided. In doing so, the mother's womb is massaged by the motion, which helps her to expel the placenta. The child can actually smell the mom's breast milk and will move toward the breasts and find them if allowed to do so, working up an appetite along the way.

The nursing mother bonds with her baby in part because of the release of a hormone called prolactin, which is produced during breastfeeding. When the baby touches the mother's nipples, yet another hormone is released, oxytocin, that causes the milk to be "let down" into the breasts. Oxytocin brings on a feeling of calm relaxation and well being in the mother.[4]

Our hormones flow through our bodies, stimulated by each successive event and brilliantly orchestrated to help us form an attachment to this new child—to love our baby, to protect it, and guide it as it grows. The biological unfolding of events works hand in hand with an emotional need to mother. We even see this in women who don't yet have children, that at a certain age they often become overwhelmed with a desire to have a child. We say, "Her clock is ticking," because built into this complex structure is a special alarm system warning of the limitations on our timing if we put off motherhood too long.

Mothering Nature

Why have we taken the time to reflect on all this? Because the design of our bodies to conceive, carry, deliver, and nurture a child is built into who we are as women. A mothering nature is native to our emotional and biological makeup. The wonders of the reproductive process are not thrown together randomly—they speak of a purpose: the nurturing of life. That's a large part of what it means to be a woman.

Let's hear from Sparkle...
Motherhood makes me whole.

In the last chapter, we spent time looking at the highest form of love. We identified greatest love as laying aside one's life for another. Who does that better than mothers? In pregnancy, they lay aside their bodies so that another can grow inside them. They sacrifice their girlish figures, their comfort, their favorite slimming

---

4. Alice Callahan, *The Science of Mom: A Research-Based Guide to Your Baby's First Year* (Baltimore: Johns Hopkins University Press, 2015).

outfits, their freedom of movement, and their future plans. As the pregnancy moves toward completion, mothers put everything else on hold to be ready for the birth of their child. In birth, they suffer terrible pain. In breastfeeding, they sacrifice their shapely breasts in favor of engorged udders that leak through their blouses. They sacrifice sleep so their babies can be fed during the night. Their entire focus shifts from themselves to the other person, who consumes their attention to the exclusion of all other concerns. As the child grows, that focus on the other is sustained over years, even throughout the life of the child.

Women who don't end up having children still have a mothering nature. Even if they have chosen childlessness, many feel that they have missed out on perhaps the most important experience that a woman can have. Some—not all—feel the lack. The blessed ones express their nature in other ways. They become that special "Auntie" to their friends' children. They excel at mentoring young people, becoming "spiritual mothers," or godmothers, or beloved teachers to many fortunate children. They lavish their mothering nature on pets or on nieces and nephews.

I love the way this commentator speaks of how the creative design of our bodies makes women bestowers of life and meaning:

> Because we are embodied creatures, women are just tied up in the fact of creation. But creation doesn't just have to be, "Oh, I had a baby." It can be...creating in the minds of children, and in the minds of other people, the meaning of life. Women are bestowers of meaning. Their strengths are not male strengths.[5]

Looking at being on the receiving end, we all need motherly love as we grow and throughout our lives. Not all of us are so blessed as to have motherly mothers. Some mothers are narcissistic and dismissive, or even abusive, of their children, acting out their own hurts on the next generation. Those of us who suffer this lack in our mothers must cope with it even as adults.

---

5. Andrew Klavan, *The Andrew Klavan Show*, episode 843, *The Daily Wire*, February 11, 2020.

A daughter's need for her mother's love is a primal driving force, and that need doesn't diminish with unavailability—it coexists with the terrible and damaging understanding that the one person who is supposed to love you without condition doesn't. The struggle to heal and cope is a mighty one.[6]

What can we learn from those mothers who fall short in expressing their mothering nature? Don't we know instinctively, even as small children, when our mothers are not living up to their role? The damage done by these mothers just makes the point that something is very wrong when a mother's natural, indwelling mothering nature is not functioning.

Un-Mothers

We've established that a woman's reproductive anatomy and mothering nature exist side by side in every woman, with potential to blossom into motherhood. Now here's the difficult part of our story: abortion deals a heavy blow to both the body and the mothering nature. In this one dreadful act the mother is undoing the natural process of life giving that was started in her body. She truncates not only the life of the child, but also the biochemical and hormonal fast-moving train her own body was on. This can't help but have ramifications for her, as her body processes the assault. The damage to the health of the body is one factor of the equation.

The other factor is that the mother has acted contrary to an essential part of who she is as a woman. The blow to a woman's identity that occurs with abortion can be likened to a racehorse that loses a leg, an athlete who suffers a disabling injury, or an artist who goes blind—except that we did it to ourselves. We were not just women having abortions. We were mothers having abortions. Abortion turned us mothers into un-mothers. A warm, protected room—as it were, the "womb room"—was prepared in-

---

6. Peg Streep, "Daughters of Unloving Mothers: 7 Common Wounds," *Psychology Today*, April 30, 2013, psychologytoday.com.

side our bodies for a child to grow to term, and into that cozy space, abortion introduced a reversal of purposes. Nurturing was exchanged for destruction. Giving life was exchanged for ending it. Self-sacrificial love, which has potential to fully blossom in motherhood, was exchanged for self-serving.

This is the deep damage done to women by abortion. Even if we move on with our lives to eventually become mothers, we carry the burden of knowing we are capable of being un-mothers. We have seen ourselves at our worst. This may result in a background noise of guilt, anxiety, or self-doubt behind our relationships with our living children.

Let's hear from Tammy...

I just always felt like, because of my prior abortion, I deserved to be rejected by my son. I imagined his rejection when it wasn't even happening. I think my insecurity really alienated him. It was clear that I was acting out something from the past that had nothing to do with him.

Our grief in abortion is a double grief: we suffer not only the loss of our child, but the loss of ourselves as mothers. What a terrible hole this leaves in our sense of self. Vacant chair, empty arms.

About Condemnation

With all this difficult self-reflection, please know that I, the author of this book, have also acted as an un-mother, so I share these complicated feelings. Yet, because of the healing process that I have gone through, I do not condemn myself or you. Why not? In a prior chapter, I spoke about the teachings of Jesus on the subject of love. As it turns out, Jesus also has something to say about condemnation. We are told of an incident involving Jesus in which a woman was caught in the very act of adultery.[7] She was brought before Jesus. Lots of angry men stood around her accusing her and ready to stone her to death, because that was the punishment the law required in those days. But Jesus said to the men, "He who is without sin among you, let him be the first to throw a stone at

---

7. John 8:7, 10–11.

her." And when he said that, all the men went away and left her alone with Jesus, because each man knew he was guilty of some sin. What did Jesus say to the woman then? "Woman, where are they? Did no one condemn you?" She answered, "No one, Lord." And finally Jesus said to this woman, "I do not condemn you, either. Go. From now on sin no more."

This woman is condemned for her wrong action and deserves death, according to the law. But she is freely offered forgiveness by Jesus. Not long after their encounter, Jesus will lay down his life as a sacrifice to pay for her sin debt, and for ours. We are guilty of our own wrongs. In violating God's morality, we suffer a fractured relationship with him—a spiritual death. We all stand condemned for falling short of his holy standard. Yet he urges us to simply believe in him, acknowledge our wrongs, and receive, as this woman did, his freely offered forgiveness. When we do so, our condemnation is lifted and our guilt is transformed into gratitude for so great a salvation.[8]

If someone in your life is condemning you, it must be that they do not know just how hard it is to go through the honest self-appraisal you're engaged in here. They must not know how committed you are to seeking peace over what has occurred, over what you've done. They may have a desire to hurt you by condemning you. For this, you might wish to consider how that condemning person might be hurting. Sometimes seeing beyond the hurt and showing a hurtful person compassion can bring peace. Please consider carefully how to handle it, as you've heard me say before that we can compound our problems by acting rashly. Take a deep breath and carry on toward your goal. Here is an opportunity to practice greatest love.

---

8. Be sure to mark the final words of Jesus to this woman who committed adultery: "From now on sin no more." On your path to peace and healing, there is no room for a future abortion, as you no doubt know full well. If you are considering abortion again, please look at adopting your child out to a loving family or keeping your child. Seek counseling from a pregnancy resource center that is not an abortion provider. You have options.

Let me remind you that you are already on the path to freedom from guilt, shame, and self-condemnation. It started with taking responsibility and confessing to God and to someone you trust. This you have already done in recounting your story in chapter 4. From there, you learned what greatest love is, and how the practice of greatest love can be applied to your child lost in abortion, righting the wrong done in the past. In the next chapter we will take time to bring a new level of honor to that child by preparing a room for him or her or them. Once you have taken responsibility, confessed, loved your child in a new way, and honored your child to the best of your ability, you will be miles closer to the freedom you seek.

Un-Fathers

Because the man is not immediately impacted by the assault of abortion on the physical body, and because the message of sex without responsibility pervades our culture, men may be spared the immediate grief that abortion brings. They can put it out of their minds more easily than the mother and go about their business without inconvenience. But over time, the primal imperative to protect his little ones that is endemic to the male identity is impacted by the realization that he has failed in his duties.

Let's hear from Jim...

I have a recurring dream where I have abandoned a woman who has a little girl. I wake up from this recurring dream with feelings of shame and guilt. Sometimes I see the little girl from a distance and long to hold her, but I know that is not possible. She is hauntingly beautiful. For a long time I did not know exactly why I was having this dream. Only after examination do I see the connection between my failure to protect my little one and the exposure of this grief coming out in the dream.

As we see from Jim's words above, although the culture allows men to be free of the responsibility of protection of the vulnerable, the overarching visceral knowledge may come to bear upon the man's psyche as he matures.

Let's hear from Kevin...

When I look at my son or daughter with pride, I sometimes have a pang for the missing one.

In the instances where men are not allowed to have a role in the decision to have the abortion, they may be left undone by a loss they couldn't control. In this case, the grief may be immediate and palpable. Not only is sex without responsibility the inheritance of modernity, but so is the notion that the decision to have an abortion should be made by the woman alone without regard to the man's desires. This is essentially emasculation.

Either way, men may seem to walk away scot-free, but they do not escape. They are impacted in many ways, some later in life as they reflect on the past. It may manifest in myriad ways, as their essential role is laid bare for them to contemplate. The little one's grip is tenacious.

Let's hear from my husband, Jerry...

There's a powerful video going around the Internet that's a compilation showing dads rescuing their children from disaster with lightening reflexes. No words could capture better than these video clips the essence of what a father is. His reflexes, keenly honed to be aware of his surroundings, react in a split second to save his child from danger. What happens when a father goes against his natural urge to protect his little one? When he turns his back and allows an abortionist to destroy his child, he will not be unscathed, no matter what he allows himself to believe. He will, in time, be confronted by his own dereliction. When he realizes what he has done, he will feel the blow to his fathering nature.[9]

So the abortion fallout makes un-mothers out of women and un-fathers out of men, alike.

---

9. Search for "Dad Reflexes Compilation" on YouTube.

Restoration!

We carry wounds. Our mothering identity is broken. How can we come back to our mothering nature after it has suffered such damage? As we look toward restoration of our mothering nature, the best place to start is with the child who suffered loss of life when we had an abortion. We will take our new understanding of greatest love and bring it to that essential relationship in the next chapter. For now, here are some questions to help you think about motherhood.

❋ What does it mean to you to be a woman (or if you're a man, what does it mean to you to be a man)? What role does motherhood (or fatherhood) play in your idea of what a woman (or man) is?

❋ Are you experiencing a crisis of identity as a mother (or father)?

❋ Is there someone in your life who is a good role model as a mother (or father)? What can you learn from her (him)?

❋ What steps can you take to allow your mothering nature to have expression?

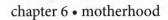

7 prepare your child's room

Then she gasped again with bewilderment and delight, for instead of the common, ugly stones she had gathered from the altars along the way, there fell into her hands a heap of glorious, sparkling jewels, very precious and very beautiful.

The last chapter ended with the idea that we can apply our new understanding of greatest love to our children lost in abortion. The progress you have made up to this point in our journey has been significant. It enables you to begin afresh with a new relationship with your children on new terms. Having made a poor parenting decision for your children in the past, how can you best parent these little ones now? What if you got a chance to love them in a new way from this moment forward?

Up until now, we have not discussed your children lost in abortion very much. Have you ever thought about loving them? What kind of love do you offer to someone you never knew—yet, at the same time, you "knew" in your body in a way only a mother can?

The love we can offer to our lost children is completely unique. However you come to love them, that quality of love will be unlike the way you love anybody else in your life—even your other children. Think about it—you are the only person your children ever knew. You were their lifeline. You held them. They had your DNA. You knew their beginning and their end—their whole story.

Set aside guilt as you think on these things. In their innocence, your children have no way of condemning or blaming you. Can you imagine loving them without carrying the unbearable burden of guilt, shame, and self-condemnation? You are ready now to transition from focusing on yourself to focusing on your children, and that includes your own guilt. Now is the time to put even self-condemnation aside as part of your practice of sacrificial giving. Self-condemnation will preserve a barrier between you and your children by keeping you focused on yourself. Hopefully, by now in our journey together, you have given plenty of thought to you already. As the parent of your children lost in abortion, take this opportunity to shift your focus to them, on loving and honoring these children as they deserve. We may be coming to this honoring late in the game, but at least we have finally arrived. It's not too late to start loving our children now.

A Second Room

The room you prepared for yourself at the outset of this journey was not a literal room, but an imaginary, conceptual room that enabled you to focus on your healing process. Similarly, you will now prepare an imaginary, conceptual room for your child. In doing so, you are making a space—in your mind, your heart, your spirit, your thoughts, your memories, your life, your family—for this other person to be remembered and honored, just as you would make space to honor the life and memory of any dear lost family member. This room is the place where your mothering nature will see restoration by your practice of greatest love toward your lost little one. It is a space that is stewarded, or managed, by you, but is for them, for cherishing, holding, embracing, honoring them. It is a marker laid down in your life that signifies remembrance of a precious person close to you who once lived.

Have you experienced the loss of a loved one before? What tools did you use to deal with your grief? In my case, when I think of the passing of my parents, I had many ways to cope with that loss. I wrote poems when my parents died. When I began a new career, I let my family know that, in doing so, I was living out qualities my father had instilled in me. I named my garden after my mom, because she always wanted for me to have a garden. I remember my parents with the lighting of a candle on the anniversary of their deaths. My remembrance of the lives of my parents is free of guilt, shame, and self-condemnation, allowing me to focus on loving and honoring them for who they were. When I became ready to honor my child lost in abortion, I composed songs about her and for her and produced a CD of the songs. That was my way of preparing a room for her.

Unlike those we memorialize who lived full lives outside the womb, these unborn children were unknown. But they were real. Like our other loved ones, our unborn children were living people full of possibility. They had beating hearts and blood flowing through their veins. And they were ours. Let your children's room be a reflection of all that you do know about them. Let it be a space set aside to celebrate the short lives of these unique individuals. Let it be an expression of your greatest love for them, arising from a mothering nature you did not have the chance to live out when you gave away the privilege of knowing and raising them. Allow your sense of loss to express itself in fully giving to the child now.

Just as we discussed ways to think about your first room, we will now discuss ways to think about your child's room.

Your child's room is an expression of your love. This room is a place of honoring and cherishing. Take your feelings and your intent to love with greatest love for this child and focus them into a constructive and creative expression. Your expression will be all your own. It may take place entirely inside the quiet of your mind and heart, or it may come forth as written words or song or planting flowers. The possibilities for expressing honor and love are limitless. If you are a creative person, you may want to make something beautiful. You might wish to make a donation to a charity in their names. Or set a landmark as a remembrance, such as planting a tree, placing a rock in a special spot, or designating a particular destination on a nature walk. You may wish to volunteer to help others who are going through the hurt of abortion as your way of giving selflessly in honor of your child.

A child's room is protected from harm. What harm could come to your lost children? They could be forgotten, minimized, or denied. What can you do in your child's room to prevent this sort of harm? In my case, my husband and I went through a season during our healing process when we adjusted our answer to the common question, "How many children do you have?" We used to answer that we have two, because we have two who are living. But during this period we changed our answer to say that we have five children—two who are living, two lost in miscarriage, and one lost in abortion. In this way, we protected our little ones from the harm of being forgotten. Have you kept your children a secret because you are keeping your abortions secret? Maybe now is the time to begin sharing this part of your life with others.

Let's hear from Tammy...

One day I was hanging out with some girlfriends, and for some reason one of them, who is a nurse, began talking about how awful abortion is. When she said that, I suddenly saw that not everyone is pro-choice, and from that moment I felt released to share my abortion stories openly.

Often, a child's room has a nameplate on the door. What are your children's names? My husband and I named all three of our lost little ones during our healing phase. This was a natural outgrowth of coming to see them as real people and coming to see ourselves as their parents. Namelessness can be the fruit of denial. Your children are real people who were part of your family, members of the generational line that you are also part of. What choice of names honors them as part of your family lineage?

Who is invited into your child's room? Others in your sphere also suffered a loss with the passing of your children. Would-be grandparents, aunts, uncles, or siblings also lost someone. Is it possible that some of them should be given access to your child's room, and, if so, what would that mean? Perhaps it means sharing with them about the journey of healing you are on. As always when dealing with others, use discretion and thoughtful consideration of their needs.

Remember that I urged you to invite God into the first room you prepared. What would it look like for you to invite God into your children's room? We can learn from the example of this mother who was parted from her child. Here is a portion of her song:

> My heart exults in the LORD; my horn is exalted in the LORD, my mouth speaks boldly against my enemies, because I rejoice in Your salvation. There is no one holy like the LORD, indeed, there is no one besides You, nor is there any rock like our God.[1]

These are the words of Hannah, mother of the ancient Hebrew prophet Samuel. Hannah says, "My heart exults in the LORD." That word *exult* in the original Hebrew, *alats*, actually means "to jump for joy." Hannah's heart jumps for joy, yet, this song is written at the moment she gives her baby away to be raised by Eli the priest. In giving her baby to the priest, she is placing him into the care of God.

Hannah copes with her grief in losing her son by shifting her focus away from her loss and onto the qualities of God that make him worth jumping for joy. She can trust him with her child because he is a God of salvation! He is holy! There is none like Him! He is a rock! Hannah's perspective enables her to have an exultant heart. What is her "horn"? It refers to the horns of bulls and other

---

1. First Samuel 2:1–2.

animals whose power and strength are carried in those majestic horns. Hannah sings that her horn, or her strength, is exalted, or raised up, in the Lord. Through the grief of the loss of our children, we are strengthened when we keep our focus on God. He enables us to rejoice even in loss, because we give our children into his loving care like Hannah did, and he is worthy to be entrusted with their care. Their spirits return to the God who gave them.[2]

Taking Action

You may wish to consider a gathering in honor of your children, either as a formal memorial service, or an informal get-together. This allows all who have been touched by the loss to come together and share in collective remembrance and grief. It also allows those who care about you to comfort you. If you have avoided speaking to your family or friends about your abortion, you have missed out on the support and compassion some may have to offer you. Or maybe you're the only one attending the memorial, taking a special moment to pay your respects in your own way.

You will find the right way to imagine and prepare your child's room that is a natural outflow of your life and circumstances. However, aside from activities and projects, the most important aspect of your child's room takes place in your heart. In preparing a room in your life for your child, you give your mothering nature a second chance to get it right. You help mend the damage done in the past by acting honorably from this moment onward. At the same time, the lost child—a real person who really lived and died—is appropriately respected and loved. Regardless of your past, you are now moving forward responsibly and motivated by a pursuit of greatest love.

---

2. Ecclesiastes 12:7: "The spirit will return to God who gave it."

Let's hear from Katie...

I have a first cousin once removed, my cousin's oldest son, who is exactly the age my child would have been, so I watch from a distance and think about what life would have been like to have raised him. Yes, I cry every once in a long while.

❀ Are you able to shift your focus off yourself and onto loving your child, without the interference caused by shame, guilt, and self-condemnation?

❀ How might your mothering nature be affected through the process of preparing a room for your child?

❀ How would you describe your child's room?

Prepare a Room

8 about sex

She paused and then added honestly and almost tremblingly, "I see the longing to be loved and admired growing in my heart, Shepherd, but I don't think I see the kind of Love that you are talking about, at least, nothing like the love which I see in you."

I'd better refresh your tea now, because this chapter is about a very difficult subject. Deep breath. The reason we need to visit the topic of sex is that this is the activity that produced a pregnancy that led to an abortion. Many choices were made along the way that brought you to where you are now. The choices come about as a result of your mindset toward your sexual nature. Let's try to understand the influences and motivations affecting your sexual life and relationships. Not all of you readers can point to sexual promiscuity as a factor in your abortion experience, but enough of you can to compel me to speak to that. Read on, even if you don't think this chapter is for you, and maybe some nugget will ring true for your circumstance.

When I have counseled unmarried young ladies hurting from abortion, I've noticed that any mild suggestion that they refrain from sex for a while causes their eyes to glaze over as though I were speaking in a foreign language. It is simply inconceivable to a sexually active young lady that she might benefit from self-restraint. I get it. I've been there myself. We have become blinded to the connection that leads from sex to baby. Yet our sexual activity led directly to our abortions. As I ponder the thousands and millions and billions of hookups taking place across the planet during this era of unbridled sexual freedom, I can't help but wonder about the casualties. How many of these hookups ended in abortion? How many women are suffering the terrible blow to their mothering nature? How many are suffering abandonment?

For you and me and the project you have undertaken in reading this book, the bottom line is that we need to heal from the hurt of abortion. In the context of our healing process, we must reevaluate our sexuality and think more deeply about what sex is in order to move forward with behaviors that are good for us rather than harmful. Can we have this conversation about our sexual choices without our eyes glazing over?

About Desire

What is desire? It is an impulse to fulfill our longings. Often, we rush headlong into trying to satisfy our desires without giving thought to where that may lead. Following our desires into sexual behaviors is particularly fraught with pitfalls. As we make decisions without thinking, based on our desires, we are sometimes confronted with consequences that surprise us. That's how many of us ended up choosing abortion. A better way to make decisions is to examine our desires and consider where they may lead, and to take control of our desires rather than being enslaved by them.

One of the first things I noticed when I started reading the bible was that it specifically speaks *against* doing what we desire:

The flesh sets its desire against the Spirit, and the Spirit against the flesh; for these are in opposition to one another, so that you may *not do the things that you please.* (Galatians 5:17, emphasis added)

Wait—you may say—*not* do the things I please? But I've always relied on "what I please" as the internal compass for my actions!

If that is you, you're in good company. That's the human story, even going as far back as Adam and Eve. There's a useful message for us in their tale. God had blessings beyond measure for humankind that required only that we look to Him rather than to our own desires. The enemy of God, knowing the pitfalls that awaited, tempted Eve to follow her desires. That enemy wanted her and wants you and me to fall into that pit. He knows that following our desires can lead us away from the blessings of God and toward trouble.

My Checkered Past

Perhaps my story will strike a chord with you. When it comes to casual sex and the problems that come from indulging our fleshly appetites without thought of consequences, I am an expert. I have lived out the excesses of the sexual revolution. I come before you—not as one who considers herself better than anyone else—but as one who has acted more foolishly and self-indulgently than most. When I got pregnant the first time, my boyfriend and I were living and sleeping together. I was in full "You go, Girl!" mode, far from home and unconstrained. Nothing stopped me from indulging every impulse. For me, it was a question of identity. I was fully identified with what I thought of as "my freedom of sexual expression." That was who I was. As I look back at it now, my "freedom" was really a form of bondage to a self-image based on a childish hunger for validation. I was a needy girl trying to fill a sense of purposelessness with something that would affirm me. And because that neediness was never filled, I kept on the same fruitless path for far too long.

I went for my abortion with about as much consideration as I would give to a teeth cleaning appointment. But one little lie that I was told at the abortion clinic led to the unraveling of a whole world of lies. They told me the procedure wouldn't hurt. That was far from the truth. The pain was overwhelming. To my horrified surprise, in the twinkling of an eye my abortion experience radically sobered me. I knew right away that I had made a horrid mistake. I was overcome with regret and rage not only toward myself, not only toward the clinic and the practitioners who terminated my pregnancy, but toward the whole thrust of indoctrination from teachers, mentors, and the culture that had so clearly lied about a woman's so-called "choice." A veil seemed to lift from my eyes, such that I could recognize what had been drilled into me since I was a young teen, when the local pregnancy center came to my high school to be sure all the girls knew how to get all the contraceptives they needed to have all the sex they wanted, and if they happened to get pregnant, they knew where to go. I suddenly saw that all this promotion of easy sex was not good for us girls. We were sold convenience, but at what cost? There were casualties involved.

I Say All That to Say This

And yet, even in the midst of this shattering moment, I still didn't know any better than to return to the same old lifestyle that had gotten me into that mess in the first place. I continued to live and sleep with my boyfriend, and I continued to indulge every impulse. Part of the lie of "choice" is that you can just get back to your life as though nothing happened. So I got back to my life as though nothing happened. One might say I was a slow learner, yet I don't think I'm unique in that. The thought of changing my behaviors—particularly sexual behaviors—was beyond my ability to conceive.

Let's hear from Melissa...

After the abortion, I went right along like nothing happened. I went for years smooth sailing. And the culture validated what I'd done. It was my body and I was going to take charge of it.

And so, it was not long—five months, to be exact—before I was pregnant once again. I do not think I am unique in this either. Without a drastic rethinking of our sexual attitudes and behaviors, women are likely to just continue barreling down the same road they were on when they got pregnant the first time. Before you know it, these women are looking back at multiple abortions. Is there another choice for them?

Conflicting Messages

The messaging about sex in our culture has many facets that conflict. On the one hand, we have the culture of casual sex, where young men and women are encouraged to explore short-term sexual hookups without commitment. We have "dating" apps to make casual sex a daily preoccupation. Both men and women find benefits to this way of relating: men get sex without responsibility, and women can pursue their lives and careers without the distraction of a relationship. Likewise, both men and women find a hazard in this culture: they don't know how to form meaningful relationships. Here are the thoughts of one current writer on hookup culture:

> If you spent those formative years (18–22) thinking that casual sex and hookups are the types of love you want and need, how else would you know what a relationship is supposed to be like? I almost never get invited out for dinner, but I get asked to "come over and watch a movie" quite frequently. Is this because men suck? Possibly. However, if that's what our culture tells young men and women dating is, it's hard to expect them to know any different.[1]

---

1. Beth Gillette, "So, I Thought Hookup Culture Ended After College...," *The Everygirl*, April 6, 2019, theeverygirl.com/hookup-culture/.

On the other hand, in the midst of the clamoring noise of the hookup option, we also hear Beyoncé reminding us that "if you liked it, then you shoulda put a ring on it." Hidden under the alluring call of the one-night stand is an ancient call that harks back to understandings of men and women coming together monogamously to prepare a stable home to welcome a child. The culture of casual sex does nothing to prepare men or women for that sort of mature commitment, yet we still long for the ancient way.

What are the roots of that ancient way, and why does it still call to us? We've discussed how women are designed for procreating and nurturing life. Men have a different sort of design that fits perfectly with women. When the two come together as husband and wife in expression of greatest love, they are joined as "one flesh," a new, perfectly designed unit composed of the two perfectly designed components, but greater than either alone. The call we feel toward this perfect union is the call of God. We may come up with our own alternatives to this design, but they will always fall short. This has been true for as long as there have been men and women, despite the siren call that seeks to undermine marriage, family, and home.

Women Acting like Men

Women today are doing things that men alone used to do not long ago, and they're outdoing men in many fields. Women fight in combat like men. Women are firefighters and police officers. Women are CEOs of major corporations. Woman superheroes in the movies can swing heavy swords and beat up all the bad guys as men swoon around them in admiration.

And women have casual sex with multiple partners like men alone used to do. What we see as the result of the sexual revolution is that women have now mastered the worst in male sexuality. Today's culture has invented a sexual option for women to hookup and walk away without any inconvenient feelings. Sort of like a female James Bond. This behavior used to be manly stuff, but now it's for everyone, and women excel at it.

At its worst, male sexuality is about the man spreading his seed without any regard for the damage done to relationships. He puts himself first, and, after he is satisfied, he forsakes his partner. He is not bound to her or to a child that comes from their union. He is more concerned with his own personal sexual freedom than with the needs of those whose lives he touches—even those whose lives he helps create. Strangely, this—the worst form of male sexuality— is the very form women are embracing today. We are encouraged to pursue sexual freedom without consequences, just like the irresponsible man. Just like them, we are encouraged to abandon our role as mothers, to abandon our children through abortion, and to forsake the building of families. This pursuit of sexual freedom that has swept women along turns them in the opposite direction from the greatest love we've learned about. Instead of lasting, committed relationships, it turns women toward temporary gratification that has nothing to do with love and leaves us unfulfilled in the long run.

King Solomon, who ought to know, because he had seven hundred wives and three hundred concubines that tragically led him astray, gave warnings we would be wise to heed:

> The lips of an adulteress drip honey and smoother than oil is her speech; but in the end she is bitter as wormwood, sharp as a two-edged sword. Her feet go down to death, her steps take hold of Sheol [the underworld]. She does not ponder the path of life; her ways are unstable, she does not know it....

> Let your fountain be blessed, and rejoice in the wife of your youth. As a loving hind and a graceful doe, let her breasts satisfy you at all times; be exhilarated always with her love.[2]

Just as commitment to a partner is contrary to the casual-sex lifestyle, so is commitment to the child that may result.

---

2. Proverbs 5:3–6, 18–19.

One product of the casual-sex lifestyle is that the more sexual partners one has, the harder it is to bond with a partner when forming a committed relationship. Here is one researcher on the subject:

> When an individual chooses to engage in casual sex, breaking bond after bond with each new sexual partner, the brain forms a new synaptic map of one-night stands. This pattern becomes the "new normal" for the individual. When and if the individual later desires to find a more permanent partner, the brain mapping will have to be overcome, making a permanent bond more difficult to achieve.[3]

Men Acting like Men

Male sexuality is one of the most powerful forces in the world. But at its highest and best, it is restrained. Rather than taking advantage, the honorable man who controls his urges respects the vulnerability of a woman's sexuality—vulnerability born of the potential consequence of pregnancy. The male sexual force blossoms into an impulse to take responsibility for creating a child. An honorable man treasures his partner and seeks her good. He "steps up" to provide for his newborn family, laying his life aside in the highest form of love. He makes a commitment to the mother of his child, so that she can feel the security to move forward in building a home. He makes sure she is cared for and protected as she does the work of mothering. He resists the temptation to sow his wild oats and brings his focus instead to the needs of his wife and child, rather than himself. His fierce sexual urges are directed to his committed partner alone, despite temptations to act otherwise. This used to be called chivalry. The wise woman encourages the redirecting of the male drive and focuses it toward stable family formation.

---

3. Pair-Bonding and the Brain, *Medical Institute for Sexual Health*, August, 2018, medinstitute.org/articles/pair-bonding-and-the-brain/.

Here is how one twenty-year-old responded to his girlfriend's pregnancy:

> I wanted to get married because I loved my wife and I wanted to devote my life to her and my kid. I wanted to be there for both of them and I wanted her there for me, and I knew that she would be. I wanted to get married basically to settle down and get some stability in my life. I wanted to quit partying and doing all the things that I did before. I just basically wanted to grow up. I felt like it was my time to grow up and to be a man and to do what was right.[4]

Women Acting like Women

In the chapter on motherhood we explored some of what it means to be a woman. We talked about how our anatomy and our mothering nature are built into who we are as women. Even for those of us who don't want children, our mothering nature enables us to practice greatest love. Loving others sacrificially gives meaning to our lives.

A woman chooses her sexual partner based on deep internal drives. Somewhere inside her, she has a sense—whether a bodily, subconscious, or real-but-buried sense—that fertilization might occur with every sexual encounter. Some part of a woman is seeking a suitable father for her potential children. The culture that divorces sex from the potential to make a baby is a culture that hates women and motherhood. The irresponsible man is part of that denial of reality, because he is seeking nothing beyond convenient sex.

One thing that distinguishes a husband from an irresponsible man is that the husband shares the risk of fertilization with his partner instead of letting her bear it alone. Husband and wife are unified. They share a united future, with or without a baby. They have a holistic view of the other—they know how other parts of

---

4. David Lapp, "Of Sex and Men: Why Sexual Restraint Matters," *Institute for Family Studies*, September 29, 2014, ifstudies.org.

their lives spill into the bedroom, and the bedroom spills into the rest of their lives. Sex between husband and wife is part of a bigger picture of two people who come together to form a third "being," called the marriage.

Let's hear from Beth...

When you marry, you are committing yourself to each other; no more sex outside of that boundary. It is like having a fire— if you make a fire in the middle of the room (sex outside of the boundaries of a committed married relationship between husband and wife), the fire will destroy the room and the whole house. But if you make a fire in the confines of a fireplace, then you will receive warmth and beauty, and nothing will be destroyed.

I so appreciate Beth's way of showing how sex as a contained passion has the power to be a beneficial presence in our lives, and, as an unrestrained passion, it has the power to destroy our lives. Again, wise King Solomon speaks similarly: "Can a man take fire in his bosom and his clothes not be burned? Or can a man walk on hot coals and his feet not be scorched? So is the one who goes in to his neighbor's wife; whoever touches her will not go unpunished" (Proverbs 6:27–29).

Sex within a committed marriage relationship is more than just a physical union that satisfies urges of the flesh. Sex is a complex of special gifts that two people give in mutuality as an expression of greatest love. It is as multi-dimensional and unique as the two individuals. What you give during sex includes your full attention, patience, respect, gentleness, humor, playfulness, protectiveness, kindness, curiosity about your partner, trustworthiness, confidentiality, and willingness to listen to the other and put your desires to the side as you consider what will bring pleasure to the other. The other person's desires become your desires, and the more you give, the more you get.

I've described the best of what sex can be between committed husband and wife according to God's perfect design. As with all things, we sometimes fall short of that ideal, even in the best marriages. If you are married, you know that it is a full-time project. I submit to you that the practice of greatest love has the power to bring your marriage to a new level. Bring greatest love to the bedroom and see what happens.

If you are still actively in the casual-sex game, how is it working for you? Are you building deep, enduring relationships? Does the future look hopeful with your partner(s)? Are you validated for who you are? If you find yourself trapped in repeated shallow encounters that are leading nowhere, it may be that this lifestyle is not a good fit for you. You must ask yourself whether the potential cost is worth the sexual freedom—and whether the sexual freedom is really freedom at all. If the answer to that question is no, then what must you do differently to ensure that you don't pay a terrible price again?

Are you willing to consider that the very best sexual experience that life has to offer a woman is with a man who has made a commitment of the highest order to her—i.e., he has given his life to be her mate so she can be secure and beloved through lifelong partnership? Marriage between a man and woman who have a commitment to each other and a God-centered focus allows for a higher experience of sex that you just can't get with partners who don't have that commitment. This is the reason some recommend "saving yourself" for marriage—because that's what is best for you! Maybe if that were your goal, and you chose not to settle for less than the best, life might open a door to a different sort of partner, one with potential to give his all to you.

If this is a season of singleness for you, perhaps you can consider drawing nearer to God during this time. The love he offers as a husband and a father to us, the sweet comfort of his presence, and the ever-deepening insights he offers into his own nature and your place in him are the greatest rewards you could possibly find in any relationship.

Before your eyes glaze over, tuck these ideas away for later contemplation.

☀ Is it time to rethink your sexual assumptions and habits? Discuss.

☀ How is your identity as a woman reflected in your sexuality?

☀ How does your understanding of greatest love intersect with your sexual identity?

9 prepare one more room

A strange new courage entered into her. She suddenly stepped forward, bared her heart, and said, "Please plant the seed here in my heart."

In this chapter, we are going to prepare one final room. But before we do, let's take a moment to look at how far you've come.

In chapter 1, you courageously set forth on this journey of peace and healing.

In chapter 2, you prepared a room, or space in your life, to focus on your healing process.

In chapter 3, you thought about how you can deal with your feelings without behaving self-destructively.

In chapter 4, you carefully told your story. You felt all the feelings, took responsibility, and gave yourself room to lament.

In chapter 5, you learned about the greatest form of love and accepted the challenge to practice loving that way.

In chapter 6, you considered your identity as a woman and the role your mothering nature plays in that identity.

In chapter 7, you prepared a special room for your children lost in abortion. In doing so, you left behind guilt, shame, and self-condemnation and restored your mothering nature by practicing greatest love toward your children.

In chapter 8, you assessed your sexual identity and reoriented toward behaviors that are good for you, rather than harmful.

Hopefully, you have already found a measure of peace and healing through these chapters. If you have found some relief, then I am pleased for you. But, if you are willing, I want to take you yet further. Early on in our time together I suggested that you could find a whole new life through this process. This is where we will develop that idea further. In this chapter, you will find the final step that can take your process to the highest level. It can make the difference between good-enough peace and healing and total peace and healing. Let me explain.

Thus far we have been speaking of things mostly in very human terms. Now, in order to access total healing, we lift our gaze beyond the human to the divine—to the spiritual dimension of our journey. We've gotten a glimpse of it through our story of the father and the rebellious daughter. We talked about how that story is a way to understand Father God and his relationship to us. Now we will go more in depth into the spiritual view of our healing process.

Humanity Is Broken

We like to think of ourselves as good. When we measure up our good deeds against our bad deeds, we hope that the good outweighs the bad. But here's the paradox: even though we try to do good, we often find ourselves failing despite our best intentions. If we were to imagine ourselves as archers shooting arrows at a target representing perfect behavior, thoughts, and attitudes, we would mostly—if not always—miss the bull's-eye.

We are not alone in this, but are part of a bigger picture of global human brokenness. We see it in our immediate circle of friends, family, and acquaintances, in the form of bad behaviors we know all too well. When we broaden our view even further to include the whole human race, is it any different? No. We see more of same, as the daily headlines prove. It's pretty hard to avoid concluding that, indeed, *no one is good*. To be human is to be broken. We are just like the rebellious daughter in our story. We want to do things our own way, and our way is slavishly bound up in this inability to hit the bull's eye. This is what is called *sin*.

We look everywhere for help—to YouTube and Google and our friends' comments on our Instagram and Facebook posts and the horoscope and the fortune cookie and the self-help book—but, for many of us, the last place we would consider looking for help is to God. When I speak of God, I don't mean just any idea of God—but rather, I am referring to the God of the Hebrew Bible, who promises abundant life, above and beyond the mundane and merely human. He offers life "in rich and unfailing exuberance."[1]

The Bible teaches us much about Father God. We learn of his grief over our sin. He created us to commune with him, but God and sin can't be in the same room. In order to be in his presence, our sin has got to go—something we don't have the power to do on our own. We can't wish it away. Why do we want to be in God's presence? Because that is where abundant life and total peace

---

1. Robert Jamieson, Andrew R. Fausset, David Brown, *Jamieson, Fausset, and Brown's Commentary on the Whole Bible* (Zondervan, 1961), at John 10:10.

and healing are found. Not being in his presence is the same as half-lived subsistence spent in darkness.

Perfect Love

Just as the rebellious daughter in our story is precious because she is precious in the father's eyes, God's love for us gives us our value. The love of even the most devoted family or friends is imperfect, but the love that comes from God is perfect love. It fills us and makes us whole as no human love can. God's love for us is not contingent on our doing good—he knows we fall short, and he has compassion on us. He sees the corruption of the world and of our own private hearts, and he loves us anyway, simply because of *who he is*, not because of anything we've done or ever could do.

God's perfect love compelled him to make a remedy to remove our sin so we could be with him. He gave his son Jesus to be manifest as perfect love in the flesh. Jesus stepped down out of heaven to commune with us in our humanness and share in our suffering and our joys. Once, Jesus called himself "the Good Shepherd," saying, "The thief comes only to steal and kill and destroy; I came that they may have life, and have it abundantly.... I lay down my life for the sheep."[2] Who are the sheep that Jesus is shepherding? You and me—we are the silly animals that make poor choices, the ones easily deceived by the thief who wants to steal our well being, kill our families, and destroy our lives. That thief, the enemy of God, has succeeded in part—he stole life and our sense of self-worth from us by his lies. But take heart! Jesus is more powerful than the thief, and his promise of abundant life still stands even now, if we are willing to say yes to it.

We have learned that the greatest form of love is to lay aside your life for others. Jesus says he lays down his life for his sheep. This refers to his death on the cross by which he took a punishment that should have come to us. We are guilty of sin and deserving of judgment, and Jesus took it in our place so we could be spared.

---

2. John 10:10, 15.

Through the sacrifice of Jesus, our sins are forgiven. Through his work, our tragedies are exchanged for blessings, our mourning for gladness, our brokenness for wholeness, our troubled hearts for hearts filled with peace. And the love doesn't stop there, because after Jesus died, he rose from the dead. By his miraculous resurrection, Jesus conquers death for us too, enabling us to enter into a timeless, eternal life of abundance with the Father.

Let's hear from Melissa...

I thought, if there is such a thing as sin, I know I have sinned by having an abortion. But God said, "Just come to me as you are, and we'll work on the details later." He brought me face to face with my sin—killing my baby—then He provided me with forgiveness. It was at this point I finally came to grips with my abortion. I took Jesus hook, line, and sinker. I know that I've sinned, and that's what brought me to the cross. I started searching for the right church, and for the first year I would just go and cry and cry and cry. I think that was part of my healing process.

Let's hear from Sparkle...

When I became a believer it helped me because I was told that God forgave me.

Let's hear from Tammy...

Part of my story is that I lost a child. God knows what it's like to lose a child too, because he suffered the loss of his son when Jesus took my sin on the cross.

Our worth is found in the one who considers us worthy of making the ultimate sacrifice. Unworthy as we are, he gives us worth. According to his assessment, we are that precious pearl of great price that was worth spending everything he had just to buy it. Jesus spent everything he had—his life—to purchase us from slavery to sin and make us his own dear possession. I am continually humbled and awed by the depth of love he has for us.

When our sins are forgiven by our heavenly Father, we find total peace because our past no longer shackles us. We are forgiven by the one whose verdict matters most. For me, self-forgiveness lost all relevance in the face of the forgiveness I received from God, because he was the one I sinned against when I took the life of his precious creation given into my care. Self-forgiveness was a place saver; God's forgiveness was the complete exoneration—however undeserved—that freed me from my sins and gave me peace.

Yet, as we read from Beth, self-forgiveness is pivotal for some in their healing process, because our self-condemnation prevents us from receiving the transformative love that God offers with his forgiveness.

Let's hear from Beth...

When I became a Christian at twenty-four, I was two months pregnant with my daughter. One of the very first things that Jesus healed me from was the abortions (aka murders) of my precious children. I learned by reading the Bible that if I called God my friend but didn't forgive myself I was calling Him a liar. I realized I needed to forgive myself because Christ forgave me! He did forgive and forget my sins and I needed to forgive myself. I did it and was set free from the horrible guilt, shame, pain, and despair of abortion. It was purely God's healing grace!

When our sins are forgiven by our heavenly Father, we find total healing because the torn places inside us are seen, held, honored, and swathed in the loving hands of the one who made us. God's embrace—his love that cradles us in his lap and gives us belonging in spite of ourselves—acts as a restorative balm on all our wounds.

One Last Room to Prepare

I invite you to prepare one last room as part of your healing process. This is a room in your heart for Jesus to live in. He is knocking at the door of your heart right now and hoping to receive an answer from anyone who hears his voice. He is offering a fresh start without the encumbrance of your past mistakes.

A commonly sung Christmas carol says, "Joy to the world, the Lord is come. Let earth receive her King! *Let every heart prepare him room.*" Here we see the global invitation to joy—that everybody on the whole earth might receive the blessings of her King—as well as an invitation to each individual—"*let every heart.*" From this lyric came the theme for our healing process. Our emphasis in this book has been on you as a unique individual with a unique story. You have thus far prepared a room for yourself and for your child. God works to transform you from the inside, from your heart. The most important room you can prepare is the one in your heart for King Jesus, who brings "joy to the world." Let *your* heart "prepare him room."

Speak to God about the room you are preparing for him. Here is one way you can do that, or use your own words:

> Thank you, Lord, for welcoming home this lost child. I come to you just as I am, broken and in need. I invite you into the room I've prepared for you in my heart, and I receive you. Lord, please forgive me for my abortions, and for all the other things I have done that weren't right. Show me who you are. Please banish the ugly presence of death from my life. Help me to learn to love like you do. Send your Holy Spirit to be my comforter and daily guide. I am ready to receive your abundant life. Thank you for making a place for me in your family.

If you have spoken these words in earnest, Jesus himself tells us that the angels are rejoicing in heaven over you right now! You are no longer lost, but found. You are enfolded into the family of God. You are cleansed of all sins of your past, and you are a new creation. I'm so happy for you! Get a Bible and read it. The Bible is where God reveals himself. He wants to be known by you. Find others who have invited Jesus into their hearts so you can grow in God's grace and knowledge.

If you have not spoken these words, you are still loved by me and—more importantly—by God. I invite you to take some time to think about these things. Consider how far you've come, and treasure any peace and healing you might have found. Don't throw away the progress you have made after all you've achieved. Perhaps you feel a tiny tug in your heart, but you have objections to Jesus. I very much understand, as I also was not willing to take that bold step until I was forty-eight years old. I felt a tug, but fought against it for a very long time. If you wish to know more about how I came to finally invite Jesus into my heart, you can read about it in the Author's Story at the back of this book.

We are about to take a look at what lies ahead as we move forward from this process you have diligently pursued. Before we do so, take a moment for these questions:

※ What sort of progress have you made thus far in healing from the hurt of abortion?

※ Have you ever considered that Jesus might play a role in your healing journey?

※ If you prepared this last room for Jesus, are you prepared to receive the total healing and forgiveness he offers?

※ If you chose *not* to prepare this last room for Jesus, can you discuss why you didn't? Can you find someone to talk to about your objections?

This song says all that needs to be said on the topic of where our worth comes from. Let it linger in your mind.

My worth is not in what I own;
Not in the strength of flesh and bone.
But in the costly wounds of love at the cross.
My worth is not in skill or name;
In win or lose, in pride or shame.
But in the blood of Christ that flowed at the cross.

Two wonders here that I confess;
My worth and my unworthiness.
My value fixed—my ransom paid at the cross.[1]

---

1. Keith Getty, Kristyn Getty, and Graham Kendrick, "My Worth Is Not in What I Own," Getty Music Publishing (BMI) and Makeway Music (Adm. by musicservices.org), 2014.

10 point of depar-ture

The first thing, however, which they realized up there on the slopes of the Kingdom of Love was how much more there would be to see and learn and understand when the King took them higher on future occasions. The glorious view which they now enjoyed was but small in comparison with all that lay beyond, and would be visible only from yet higher places above.

I notice the shadows are lengthening, and the day is getting on. The teapot has cooled. I know you need to be on your way soon. But before we say goodbye, let's talk about where you go from here. Let's share some final thoughts about how to use this moment as a point of departure. I have the highest hopes for your future. I foresee for you a life of freedom from the burdens of the past. I see restored relationships and insight about your healing process that deepens throughout your life. I see you drawing nearer to God and discovering the wealth of blessing that comes from being his beloved child. So much goodness is before you. You have every reason to be hopeful.

The Right Time to Act

Throughout these chapters I have been urging you not to take action involving others because of the potential for creating new problems during a time when you are particularly raw and vulnerable. I know how tempting it can be to react rashly to our strong emotions. Sometimes the hardest thing in the world is to *not* act. In seeking what is best for you, I recommended you wait to act until you've had time to gain perspective.

Once you have gained that perspective, where interpersonal action is called for, I encourage you to let greatest love be the guiding principle in all your actions. Be willing to lay your needs aside for the benefit of others. Consider that your words and actions might hurt others rather than help them. This becomes a great measuring tool. In any specific instance, if you find you can't act out of greatest love, that means it's not good to act at all. It's kind of like when your mother told you, "If you can't say something nice, don't say anything at all." That advice holds here. If you can't add constructively to a relationship, then keeping silent may be best. You will benefit from a trusted friend or mentor who can bring wisdom to you as you consider your options.

How might you act once you're ready? You may wish to consider the following:

- Telling someone who needs to know that you had an abortion

- Listening to others who were affected by your abortion, giving them an opportunity to express their feelings

- Asking forgiveness from those you hurt along the way

- Extending forgiveness to those who hurt you along the way

- Sharing with someone about your healing process

- Activities of remembrance for your lost child, as discussed in chapter 7

- Reaching out to help others hurting from abortion

Making Amends

One of the great benefits of learning to practice greatest love is that it makes apologizing when we do wrong much easier. When we shift the focus from our pride to the person we have wronged, we begin to see them more compassionately. We become more willing to admit our mistakes to them and ask their forgiveness, because we want to honor them more than we want to save face. This process can have powerful healing effects for both parties. Sometimes, however, the other person doesn't want to accept your apology and forgive you. Respect that person's limits and step away. All you can do is make your best attempt; the results are never guaranteed.

Sometimes an apology is not enough. You may need to take some restorative action—something that goes beyond words to right a wrong. Going even further, you may even need to begin living differently. For example, do you remember Crystal, the girl I met with in the park? She was raging at her boyfriend to cover up feelings about her multiple abortions. She needed to make a big change in her life to correct what had become for her a habit of abusive behavior.

How about the people who wronged you? Don't they owe you an apology? You can't force someone to see their wrongs and ask your forgiveness—their journey is their own. But in some cases, you may be able to share your experience with them in a way that opens their eyes to the hurt they caused. I can tell you that a gentle, non-confrontational approach is more likely to be effective than hurling accusations. Speak about you, not about the other person. Again, no guaranteed outcomes. By keeping your focus on your path, you can come to a point in your healing where you will be able to forgive them regardless of their attitude toward what they did. This can happen without their involvement in your process. You may never see that person again. They may not be living. But you can forgive them. Withholding forgiveness hurts you, not the other person. Bitterness and resentment eat away at you, and they're addictive. They arouse feelings of righteous indignation that lead to pride and self-pity, driving you further and further away from the humility of greatest love. The sooner you kick that nasty habit, the better for you.

In all cases, I strongly urge you not to take action in these important interpersonal matters without praying about them and reading the bible beforehand. Just talk to God and ask him to help you. Very often our bible readings bring insight to our circumstances, sometimes in the most extraordinary ways. We read that God's Word is living, active, and able to judge the thoughts and intentions of the heart. You may find the answers to your prayers right there on the page.

Revisiting Your Room

The three rooms you prepared in the course of this book remain with you as places of refuge, reflection, and relief. Each in its own way has something to offer in the long term. The room you prepared for yourself as you embarked on this process will always be a testament to all you've accomplished. You secured it against interference, and you used it as the place for your story to safely unfold. You furnished it with the things you needed to find comfort through challenges. Instead of running away, you showed up there for the benefit of your own well being. It enabled you to face difficult truths, learn from them, and honor your unique life experience. That room is yours, and it is to be cherished.

You may not be done processing the effects of abortion and the mental, physical, spiritual, and emotional toll it has taken. Know that the courage you have displayed thus far will carry you through. If you have more grieving to do, you know where to go and how to honor your tears. For most of us, our understanding of the abortion continues to change its shape throughout our lives. It looks different as our vantage point shifts. Parenthood, other losses, divorce, disappointment, menopause, aging, and lots of other life markers affect how we see it. When we are in the midst of these various changes, we may have difficulty perceiving how this healing work is affecting our lives. But in hindsight, it will be easier to discern. We may go through seasons when we don't think about our abortion at all, and suddenly it resurfaces—who knows why. Leave a space for continued contemplation, new insights, and new commitments.

As you reflect on all you've learned, consider how your practice of greatest love will be the key to lead you toward positive change in your relationships and life decisions. It will enable you to cease being motivated by selfishness and instead develop discipline, thoughtfulness, and a forgiving nature. That's the difference between a child and a grownup. The mature person can "Go low, Girl!" and diffuse problems rather than having to compound them with impulsive, reactive behaviors. Practicing greatest love will make you a better friend, spouse, parent, sibling, and child—even a better stranger to those you happen to meet and to whom you may extend yourself. Your example will help those around you to make the leap with you to a better way of love. Take small steps to develop the habit of laying yourself aside for others—not as a doormat, but as one who willingly chooses to focus on the needs of others over yourself as an expression of your highest self. And when you blow it, just tell God all about it and get back on track.

Revisiting Your Child's Room

The room you prepared for your child will always be a testament to the unique individual who was once a part of you and is now lovingly remembered and honored. That room is a memorial to a dear loved one who is a permanent part of your life. It is fueled by pure love—free of guilt, shame, and self-condemnation. It allows you to honor by remembering.

You recognized how your initial treatment of your unborn child caused damage to your mothering nature. Your child's room is the place you found your mothering nature restored, because there you took the opportunity to get it right in how you love your little one. Peace comes from righting that wrong.

How can you go further on this path, as you orient yourself toward being a help to others? Isn't it likely there are other women in the same shoes you were in when you began seeking relief from the hurt of abortion? Do you know someone who would be helped by learning from what you've been through in your healing process? Are you willing to speak openly with another about this topic that you might have once fought tooth and nail to keep secret? One way to lay aside your life for another is to overcome the discomfort of going public for the sake of helping another hurting person.

Revisiting the Room in Your Heart

The room you prepared in your heart for Jesus will always be a testament to God, who made you, knows you, loves you, forgives you, and has the power to turn you from the mistakes of the past toward a future and a hope. This room will continually grow and expand, taking you to new heights and depths of insight about who God is and who you are in light of him. Your life matters to him. He will never leave you or forsake you, but will dwell in your heart forever. He will be your friend, comfort, guiding light, and source of lasting joy. In this room, you will discover your life purpose, which is not found in anything you do, but in being in the presence of the one who did everything and gave his all for you. He is worthy of an eternity of thanks and appreciation.

This third room is the most important of the three rooms, as it is the life of Jesus *in* you. It daily nourishes you with the love of Jesus and has eternal impact. It carries you through all the years and phases and seasons of your life. Then, even after your life is over, it still impacts you. After death, Jesus carries you with him to a timeless place of peace in a heavenly kingdom, where your unborn children dwell even now. Perhaps we will be reunited with our unborn loved ones in that place. That will not be a shameful meeting—it will be a joyful reconciliation, because his kingdom is marked by forgiveness. Every tear there is wiped away by God himself, and there is no death, sorrow, crying, or pain.

Still One More Room

You have prepared three rooms. What you may not know is that God is preparing a room for you even now. Here is how Jesus expresses it:

> There are many dwelling places in my Father's house. Otherwise, I would have told you, because I am going away to make ready a place for you [Yes, you read that right—Jesus is *preparing a room* for you!]. And if I go and make ready a place for you, I will come again and take you to be with me, so that where I am you may be too.[1]

We can come to a fuller understanding of these words of Jesus by exploring the Hebrew marriage traditions of his time. Unlike today, in his era, it was customary for a man to travel from the house of his father to seek a wife. He would pay a bride price to the bride's father and then exchange a glass of wine with his betrothed to seal the betrothal. When the man and woman became engaged, that engagement was considered as unbreakable a commitment as being married. The man would then head back to his father's house to prepare a place for his bride to come and live with him. This period of preparation lasted a year or so. The bride did not know exactly when to expect her groom to return for her. So, she waited expectantly and always in a state of readiness, with the assurance that when he did come back, he would take her to a house and home in which she would find a place—a room, as it were—carefully prepared just for her.

We can think of ourselves as the expectant bride of Jesus. He came looking for those who would believe in him, like a groom

---

1. John 14:2–3 NET.

seeking out a bride. He paid the bride price with his blood and body on the cross. He sealed a new covenant with a cup of wine, which is the origin of what we know now as the communion, or Eucharist. After his death and resurrection, he went back to his father's kingdom and promised before he left—in the words we read above—that he was preparing a place for us and would come back to bring us to himself. At one point in the bible, we are able to eavesdrop on Jesus as he is speaking to Father God. He says this: "Father, I want those you have given me [that's us!] to be *with me where I am*, so that they can see my glory that you gave me because you loved me before the creation of the world."[2] We are waiting for his return. We don't know when it will be, but we stay ready at every moment.

You need never again experience a sense of not belonging. You belong in the special place being lovingly prepared for you by God's son in his father's house. Jesus considers you his precious, beloved bride—men and women alike—all who believe in him. There is a place in God's house, a place at God's dinner table, a place in God's family for you. Imagine a room prepared just for you by the richest, most loving husband who ever lived!

God Be With You

Thank you for spending this special time with me. You've given so much of yourself. I really appreciate you, and I will keep you in my prayers. I hope we'll have tea together again one day. Feel free to stay in touch. I can be reached at PrepareARoom.com. Please take with you some of my special tea blend as a memento of our time together. I know that whenever I drink it, I will think of you.

> *And indeed if they had been thinking of that country from which they went out, they would have had opportunity to return. But as it is, they desire a better country, that is, a heavenly one. Therefore God is not ashamed to be called their God; for He has* prepared a city *for them.* (Hebrews 11:15–16)

---

2. John 17:24 NET, emphasis added.

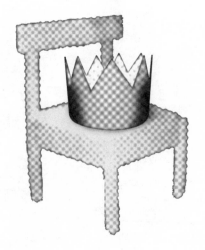

epilogue: foundlings

The child my husband and I aborted is the central character in the story of how I found peace and healing. Although the forgiveness of Jesus was offered to me, I could not accept it. I was willing to receive divine forgiveness for what I considered lesser sins, but when I thought about the child I destroyed, I was paralyzed with guilt.

One day, I cried out in anguish, "How can I find forgiveness after what I've done to my child?" An answer came back to me that took the form of a new understanding. Let me share it with you.

I read in the Bible that our aborted children go to a heavenly dwelling place to live with God.

> The dust will return to the earth as it was, and the spirit will return to God who gave it. (Ecclesiastes 12:7)

> My father and my mother have forsaken me, but the LORD will take me up. (Psalm 27:10)

In that heavenly place, there is joy. There are no tears, no pain, no mourning.

> In Your presence is fullness of joy. (Psalm 16:11)

> He will wipe away every tear from their eyes. (Revelation 21:4)

Our lost children live securely in the perfect, comforting lap of the One who *is* forgiveness. That One is Jesus. He knows how we have sinned—including our abortions—and He knows that we can't possibly bear the burden of our sin debt, which has come up as a barrier between us and God. To help us, He paid our sin debt Himself, dying on a cross so we could be free and have eternal life with Him.

I said yes to Jesus. The forgiveness that Jesus extended was and is sufficient. To me, it was as though my child were responding to my anguished cry with the words, "I'm with Jesus! How can I help but forgive you?" The burden of guilt lifted off my shoulders.

When I began to think about the vast countless numbers of aborted babies living in the heavenly lap of Jesus,[1] I set out to draw one child each day as my way of honoring them, presenting them as they might appear if they had lived.

Today's culture has severed the link between our actions and their consequences in the area of reproduction—between sex and baby. These winsome sketches personalize the consequences of our actions. They give a face to the "clump of cells."

The drawings are the product of my imagination, but I can declare with certainty that our real aborted children are beloved of God, and they are citizens of a joyful eternal kingdom where sin has been overcome, and where love reigns.

I call the collection Foundlings. The word *foundlings* refers to infants abandoned on doorsteps, to be found by others who might care for them. We once abandoned our little ones, and God found them on His doorstep. He fills in the gaps where our love once fell short. But now that we know how to love them with the greatest love, we can embrace them as God does, with full assurance that we are forgiven by Him and by them.

My hope is that these wee ambassadors of God's grace and forgiveness serve to invite you closer to Jesus.

---

1. Fr. Shenan Boquet, "1.72 billion abortions worldwide in the last 40 years," *LifeSite*, April 1, 2013, lifesitenews.com. Dr. Brian Clowes, director of education and research at Human Life International, estimates that 1.72 billion babies have been aborted worldwide in the last forty years.

You can find many more Foundlings and purchase full-color
signed giclée Foundling prints at PrepareARoom.com.

a parting gift

The words of the Bible provide the perfect way to think and pray about the process you've been going through. As a parting gift for you, I have selected ten Bible verses that correspond to the ten-part journey you have just taken, along with some thoughts on how you might use them in contemplation and prayer.

1 ~ Hello

> **Psalm 23:4.** *Even though I walk through the valley of the shadow of death, I fear no evil, for You are with me; Your rod and Your staff, they comfort me.*

When we read the words, "You are with me," we think of one of the names of the Messiah: Immanuel, a name meaning "God with us." As you step out on the path to peace and healing, it may seem like you are on the most lonely journey imaginable. But the Good Shepherd is with you, walking by your side, gently leading, guiding, and protecting His little lamb. His eye is on the destination He has for you, and He knows the paths of righteousness and the places of green pasture and still water along the way. He also knows you can't achieve your destination without going through dark valleys. He is with you during those dark times, showing His steadfast presence with a rod of correction and a staff of reassurance. How comforting to know you are looked after so tenderly!

The destination the Shepherd has in mind for you is nothing less than His own house, where you will live with Him forever.

2 ~ Prepare a Room

> *Psalm 71:1–3. In You, O Lord, I have taken refuge;*
> *Let me never be ashamed.*
> *In Your righteousness deliver me and rescue me;*
> *Incline Your ear to me and save me.*
> *Be to me a rock of habitation to which I may continually come;*
> *You have given commandment to save me,*
> *For You are my rock and my fortress.*

The Lord, our Father God, is a room to which we can continually come. He is a permanent rock of habitation—an impenetrable place of refuge as strong as a fortress. In this space, shame cannot enter. The ear of the Lord is inclined toward you as you pour out your heart to Him in the shelter of His salvation.

3 ~ Time to Stop

Luke 15:20–24. But while he was still a long way off, his father saw him and felt compassion for him, and ran and embraced him and kissed him. And the son said to him, "Father, I have sinned against heaven and in your sight; I am no longer worthy to be called your son." But the father said to his slaves, "Quickly bring out the best robe and put it on him, and put a ring on his hand and sandals on his feet; and bring the fattened calf, kill it, and let us eat and celebrate; for this son of mine was dead and has come to life again; he was lost and has been found." And they began to celebrate.

We rebellious children were once foolish, disobedient, deceived, and enslaved to various lusts and pleasures. God loved us even then. The moment we become self-aware and willing to turn from our foolishness and toward our heavenly Father for mercy and renewal, He saves us, not on the basis of our deeds, but according to His mercy. He removes our filthy, road-weary tatters, and He clothes us in His finest robe and a ring that identifies us as members of His family. The love of our heavenly Father transforms us from lost orphans to royal heirs.

4 ~ What Happened

*__Isaiah 61:1–4.__ The Spirit of the Lord G*OD *is upon Me, Because the* L*ORD has anointed Me to bring good news to the afflicted; He has sent Me to bind up the brokenhearted, to proclaim liberty to captives and freedom to prisoners;*
To proclaim the favorable year of the L*ORD and the day of vengeance of our God; to comfort all who mourn, to grant those who mourn in Zion, giving them a garland instead of ashes, the oil of gladness instead of mourning, the mantle of praise instead of a spirit of fainting. So they will be called oaks of righteousness, the planting of the* L*ORD, that He may be glorified. Then they will rebuild the ancient ruins, they will raise up the former devastations; and they will repair the ruined cities, the desolations of many generations.*

What happened to us is no surprise to God. Before the foundation of the world He already had a remedy in place to deal with it—to bind up our broken hearts and free us from our captivity to the past. That remedy was a man sent from the heavenly kingdom to live as one of us. God put His Spirit on that man and anointed Him. The man Jesus brings good news about awesome exchanges He is able to bring about: He gives us gladness in exchange for our mourning, praise for our fainting; ruined lives are rebuilt, generations of desolation are repaired. He transplants us from our paltry dust into His rich earth. As His planting, we become mighty oaks of righteousness, and our spreading branches bring Him glory.

5 ~ What Is Love?

Mark 10:45. *For even the Son of Man did not come to be served, but to serve, and to give His life a ransom for many.*

We look to Jesus as the model for sacrificial love. In all He did, we see His humility in action. Instead of a palace, God Himself chose a place of birth among farm animals, where He was laid to rest in a feeding trough. God Himself kneeled down and washed the feet of the disciples. God Himself suffered the most humiliating death on a cross, to take the judgment that we deserved, as the ransom for our sins. God Himself was willing to be our servant, even to death. Following His example, we are called to step off our self-made thrones and empty ourselves, putting pride to death and giving ourselves entirely away as a living sacrifice. This is the opposite of what we are inclined to do, so it requires thoughtful, deliberate, prayerful intention. Lord, help us to be servants like You!

6 ~ Motherhood

Romans 8:33–34. *Who will bring a charge against God's elect? God is the one who justifies; who is the one who condemns? Christ Jesus is He who died, yes, rather who was raised, who is at the right hand of God, who also intercedes for us.*

Jesus not only died for us and was raised, but made it His ongoing, present-tense task to intercede on our behalf before Father God.

With the greatest lawyer of all time defending us, none can bring a charge against us—none can condemn us. Lord, we ask You to take away our self-condemnation and help us to know that, in all things, we are conquerors because of Your love for us.

7 ~ Prepare Your Child's Room

Psalm 34:1–5. I will bless the Lord at all times; His praise shall continually be in my mouth. My soul will make its boast in the Lord; The humble will hear it and rejoice. O magnify the Lord with me, and let us exalt His name together. I sought the Lord, and He answered me, and delivered me from all my fears. They looked to Him and were radiant, and their faces will never be ashamed.

When we keep the praise of the Lord continually in our mouths, we keep our focus on our source of life rather than on ourselves. This is an invitation not only to rejoice in the Lord, but to invite others to join you in a community of praise where you can "exalt His name together." Every individual in that community has their own story of how God "answered me," and "delivered me," just like the Jewish slaves were answered by God and were delivered from bondage. In the light of His radiance, our faces shine.

8 ~ About Sex

Isaiah 55:1–3. Ho! Every one who thirsts, come to the waters; And you who have no money come, buy and eat. Come, buy wine and milk without money and without cost.
Why do you spend money for what is not bread, and your wages for what does not satisfy? Listen carefully to Me, and eat what is good, and delight yourself in abundance. Incline your ear and come to Me. Listen, that you may live.

We have sought to fill a thirst within us with things that cannot satisfy. We have "spent" our attentions on relations that leave us unnourished and starving. We are being called to "come" to that freely given water, wine, and milk. The water is Jesus, the Living Water that becomes a spring of water gushing up to eternal life in us, by His grace. The wine is His blood shed for our sins. The milk is the Word of the Bible, that nourishes and grows us in Him, even as a mother's milk nourishes her growing baby. "Listen, that you may live!" Having squandered our lives to the point of bankruptcy, let us now spend ourselves on God, for He satisfies as life-giving nourishment.

9 ~ Prepare One More Room

Ephesians 1:6 (*KJV*). *To the praise of the glory of His grace, wherein He hath made us accepted in the Beloved.*

Accepted in the Beloved. What a beautiful picture of where we dwell with Jesus. Our heavenly Father has taken this wayward, rebellious child and made a way for us to be enfolded in His loving arms. Jesus is God's Beloved, and He is our Beloved as well. There is no more comforting place to be than in the Beloved. For this gift of belonging, of acceptance, of greatest love bestowed on us, we proclaim the glory of His grace and praise Him forever.

10 ~ Point of Departure

Revelation 3:20−21. Behold, I stand at the door and knock; if anyone hears My voice and opens the door, I will come in to him and will dine with him, and he with Me.
He who overcomes, I will grant to him to sit down with Me on My throne, as I also overcame and sat down with My Father on His throne.

Patiently, generously, graciously, the Savior awaits our readiness to answer His knock. He is willing to leave aside the privilege of His divine station, just to sit and share a meal in covenant with us. Jesus gives us a glimpse beyond the limits of our earthbound life to our place in the heavenly realm, and—to our utter amazement—we find we are given the unspeakable honor of sitting with Him on His throne. Saying yes to Jesus is the point of departure for an extraordinary, limitless new life. I am so excited for your continuing journey!

the author's story

My sister and I grew up in a secular Jewish home in San Francisco. My grandparents on both sides were cosmopolitan Europeans who had no interest in Jewish religious practice. Yet they instilled in my parents a strong Jewish cultural identity. My father's family immigrated to the U.S. from Rumania at the end of the nineteenth century, settling in New York along with so many of that generation.

My mother was raised in Vienna, Austria, and escaped the Nazi Holocaust with her family by fleeing to the West Indies island of Trinidad in 1938, just months after the Nazi incursion into Austria, an event called the Anschluss. Imagine the culture shock when the family was forced to walk away from everything they knew—their sophisticated middle-class life, my grandfather's business, their apartment in the very heart of Vienna a block from the bustling arts center of the city, all their belongings and friends—and begin their lives over again on a remote tropical island. Mother spent her teenage years and early twenties with her family—seven years in all—living mostly in a British internment camp in Port of Spain, Trinidad, with other refugees fleeing the war.

My father was an American soldier stationed in Trinidad. Mother and Father met, discovered they had in common a love of art, and prepared to wed. The whole family resettled in New York City with my father's help. Both my parents had studied art, and after Dad's army career ended, they came out to the wild west—San Francisco—to pursue a life dedicated to the arts and to grow their family.

San Francisco in the mid-twentieth century was a place of jazz clubs, beat poets, and lifestyle experimentation. My parents were Bohemians who taught fine-art painting and made art. I was encouraged to follow in their footsteps and express myself creatively in every way from a young age. When I was four, my parents bought a church and converted it into our house, at a period when that sort of conversion was unheard of. They removed the cross from the window and the pews from the main hall and repurposed the place for the worship of art. And to put a cherry on top of our Church of Art, my father told me as a small child that he was God. And I believed him. He was a perfectly delightful god to me. I did feel drawn to participate in Jewish observance because of our occasional attendance at our friends' Passover Seders, but Dad had contempt for religion, and he discouraged me. He reveled in his irreverence and brought it into his art and his parenting. Such was the atmosphere of my upbringing.

Not surprisingly, my parents' marriage did not survive the freewheeling spirit of the times. Their divorce broke our family apart when I was ten, leaving me alone, a young girl living unsupervised in the crazy sixties of Berkeley, California. The era of my youth was a time of tearing down traditions and questioning authority. All with whom I came in contact explored unorthodox ways of being, further cementing my counter-culture mindset. I graduated early from high school so I could cast out on my own. I went to college and at the same time dove headlong into a self-guided tour of every sort of unbridled indulgence that life had to offer. My life consisted of following my urges without restraint.

My parents, the pervasive feminist movement, and the general rebellious culture of the day all conspired to point me toward a deep dive into sexual activity. I had many sexual encounters and never thought twice about it. It was simply how things were done then.

The Abortion

After college, I met a man that I liked very much, and we immediately began living and sleeping together. I got pregnant. We both thought nothing of it. I made an appointment for an abortion, and my boyfriend didn't even bother to come with me to the appointment. That's how little we thought of the process—like it was no different from a dental checkup. I was taught that I had a right to an abortion. That must mean it's a good thing. I was proud to finally be getting around to the signature act that defined independent young women. I only knew *my* body, *my* choice, *my* future, *my* life.

At the clinic, I paid money and sat in a circle with other ladies who were to have abortions that morning. This was a mandatory "counseling session." Each woman in the circle took a turn explaining why she was there. No one made any response to any of the women. It was just a silly formality. I remember how flippant I was—I couldn't take the whole thing seriously—I remember this because that flippant attitude was about to get a rude slap in the face.

A young attendant led me into a private room where I took off my clothes and put on a paper gown. The abortionist came in, and I piped up and asked him if it would hurt. He said no. The truth of what I experienced moments later shocked me. The pain was excruciating. I had never experienced pain like that in my life before. It put me into a sort of shock. When the procedure was over I was told to get dressed. I was clearly upset. After the abortion, neither the abortionist nor the attendant would make eye contact with me any more. Something about me and my emotional reaction made them very uncomfortable. I stumbled back into my clothes and headed out toward the front to leave. But the attendant stopped me. She shuffled me instead out the back door, where I exited down a metal staircase something like a fire escape. They didn't want the girls up front to have to see someone coming out upset. That might discourage good, paying customers.

I stumbled to the parking lot. I could hardly find my car for the tears bursting out of my eyes. I knew immediately that I had done something very wrong. I felt so alone. I was torn up, and felt betrayed by all I had been taught regarding my sexual freedom and my right to an abortion. Rage, regret, and despair coursed through me, though I did not give much thought at that time to the child that had just vanished from my body. I still thought only of myself.

As I approached my car, a colorful object on the ground caught my eye through the tears. It was an old, dented metal lapel pin that looked like it had been run over by a thousand cars. I stooped to pick it up and held it in my hand. It pictured a mother bird with her wings stretched over her chicks. The words beneath the picture read, "He careth for you." I reasoned that it had to be God speaking because of the word "careth"—in my naivete, I thought, of course God speaks in King James English. At that darkest moment, I felt the hand of the *real* God—not the god of my childhood—reach down out of heaven to touch me with comfort. This was the "arm of God" we read about so often in the Hebrew Scriptures and see in the Passover, known in Hebrew as the *zeroa*. I clung to that message. I took it personally. God actually seemed to know my pain and to go out of his way to tell me he "careth" for me. That was my first encounter with God, and it was a lifeline during a dark time and has continued to be so ever since.

The Almost-Abortion

My boyfriend and I didn't know any better than to continue living and sleeping together just as we had, and within a matter of months, I was pregnant again. I made another appointment at another clinic. By this time we were in Corpus Christi, Texas, the city named after the Body of Christ. This time things were different. I still felt I had to abort, but I wasn't sure why. My boyfriend spent the whole night prior to the abortion appointment sick in the bathroom. We got no sleep, as his body was violently purging out both ends. Was this his body telling him that something terribly wrong was about to take place? In the morning, as we drove up to the clinic, I noticed a group of women off to the side of the building quietly praying together as they watched me go in.

My boyfriend waited in the car. Again, I went in and paid the money. But a strange thing happened this time. The abortionist was kept occupied with whatever he was doing for an extra hour or so after my scheduled appointment time. As I sat there during that hour, I weighed my options. Sitting with the circle of women at my first abortion appointment, the ringing directive about my "right to an abortion" consumed all my attention so that there was no room for thoughtfulness. But now I sat alone. Life seemed to be on pause. In that silence I was able to perceive a small, quiet voice coming from inside me, the voice of someone who was mysteriously alive. I thought about the desolation I'd felt after my first abortion. I wondered if I had the courage to change my plans and adjust my path to raise a child on my own. I didn't know the boyfriend all that well, but I knew that if he didn't want to be a father, I could go back home to San Francisco and get help from my parents in raising the child on my own. Slowly and gradually, I began to entertain the thought of being a mother.

Just as I was approaching the front desk to cancel my appointment and get my money back, my boyfriend rushed in the door. He had been doing some serious thinking too. "You didn't do it, did you?" he cried. "Come on, let's get out of here!" We rushed out the door and sat in the car in the parking lot of the abortion clinic in Corpus Christi, Texas. There, he proposed to me, and I accepted. We drove off with big grins on our faces, into the unknown future, but willing to let that unknown include a child.

In some ways, it's harder to have had an almost-abortion than an abortion. This is because I have a constant reminder of what I came so close to destroying, which points directly to what I did destroy. This second person that grew inside of me became the start of a small family. My boyfriend and I married, and my wedding dress accommodated a hugely pregnant belly. Our son was born, and we later had a wonderful daughter. Still later, we lost two more children in miscarriages.

Our son excelled, and continues to excel, in everything he puts his hand to. He is a continual reminder of the preciousness of life. He aimed high in his career goals and, even as a young man, has already achieved great things. He now has a family, with five children of his own.

During the pregnancy with our son's youngest child, medical issues arose that concerned everyone for the baby's life. The doctors recommended that my son and his wife consider aborting the child. That was inconceivable to them. They would make room in their lives for this child regardless of his medical condition. And they have done so. The child is a miracle baby who brings joy and gives glory to God just by his very existence. My daughter-in-law wrote a song to honor her miracle child. Here are some of the lyrics:

You have less, so God can give more.
This lesson we've been shown before:
Gideon knows what can be done,
When we show trust, our war is won.

God left a bit of clear blue sky
In the corner of your right eye.
That's insurance enough for me.
I'm standing back so I can see

All the glory He wants to show
In this sweet boy I'm watching grow.

Our daughter's story is also precious. Her path mirrors mine in some ways, in that she became pregnant out of wedlock. But she would not consider terminating her pregnancy, so the child she carried became the start of her family. Little Naomi transformed us into grandparents, and our daughter and her boyfriend married. Now they have six children. As my boyfriend-turned-husband and I look at our two amazing children and our eleven grands, we declare victory over the spirit of death that once had a grip on our family, but whose grip has evaporated by the work of the Holy Spirit of God.

My husband and I consider the explosive growth of our family a remarkable turn of events for ones such as us. We are the most unlikely candidates for such an abundance of family. Yet, this is the blessing that God has chosen for us, in spite of ourselves.

Miraculous Encounter

Although my boyfriend was not behaving in a very Christian manner when we met, he always treasured his relationship with Jesus. He was a "PK," or preacher's kid, and had been raised in a god-fearing, Christian home. But, as with many PKs, he leapt like a tightly wound spring out of that godly environment into a life of abandon. Along the way, he and I collided and began our family. As he transitioned from a hell raiser into a responsible father, he began to return to his Christian faith. This was very difficult for me as a Jew, as I had many prejudices about Christians. I requested that he refrain from speaking to me about Jesus. That name was just too jarring for my Jewish ears, like fingernails on a chalkboard. He began to pray for me, and he prayed for twenty-two years, until one day I had a miraculous encounter with Jesus myself.

My encounter took place in a church on an Easter Sunday morning. I would not attend church regularly with my husband, but I did make an allowance for one day a year for him: Easter. I was at this particular service because my husband bribed me to go with an offer of lunch at a nice restaurant afterwards. He had bought me a cute frock and this would be my chance to show it off. That was where my thinking was that morning.

For many years I had thought about God. Since my first encounter in the parking lot outside the abortion clinic, God had been gently leading me and coaxing me to himself. Because of my husband's faith, I wrestled with whether or not I could have a relationship with God without having to "do the Jesus thing." At the time of this Easter service, I was suffering from an intrusion of uncontrollable and haunting thoughts that I would one day cause the death of children. Now I see that these thoughts sprang from the ugly, deadly seed planted by my abortion experience, the destructive work of the enemy of God—the thief. I didn't understand then. That day at the Easter service, when the pastor told the congregation to close their eyes and "invite Jesus into your heart," I was thinking of those haunting thoughts. Somehow I just knew that Jesus would take them away. I don't know how I knew with such certainty, but that small bit of faith was just enough to propel me to take the most uncomfortable and foreign step imaginable. I invited Jesus into my heart, through gritted teeth, as one defeated. How could I know that it would be the best thing that ever happened to me? At the moment of my reluctant invitation, Jesus did pour into my heart, like a shower of golden honey. I was overcome by the beauty of what was entering into my heart. I was instantly transformed, rewarded with a certainty that not only would the haunting thoughts cease, but that a whole new world I could never have imagined was now opened to me. Death was conquered; I had been given a new life. My experience was immediate, undeniably transformative, and irreversible. I have not been the same since that moment.

Unforgivable Sins?

I knew as I embarked on this new relationship with God's son Jesus that I carried a great sin in my past. I measured my sin of abortion as among the worst things that a person can do. How in the world could I accept the beautiful gift of forgiveness for that horror? Jesus forgives our sins, but I could not give him that one. I began to seek God about this dilemma, attending worship services in churches all over my county—whenever there was a meeting of any sort, any day of the week, I was there. I just cried and cried out for relief.

One day something very strange happened. I'm not sure I can explain it adequately. It involved an animated character that I invented, that had been living in my imagination for years. As a trained animator, this was not unusual, as I have animated many characters. This particular character was a little girl with black pigtails. I made up stories about her and drew her. She became a constant companion—sort of an imaginary friend. During my period of seeking God's forgiveness for my abortion and my almost-abortion, I seemed to hear from this imaginary little girl, as though she had come to life on her own. She seemed to ask me, "Don't you know who I am?" I understood at that moment that I had created this character as a placesaver for the child I lost in abortion. The message she seemed to convey to me was one of forgiveness, as though she were witnessing my dilemma. She could not help but forgive me for taking her life, because she was living in the lap of the one who is forgiveness incarnate—Jesus himself.

From that time on, I have not been concerned with forgiving myself, or feeling unforgiven. The only forgiveness that matters to me is what Jesus offers, and I accept his forgiveness as applied to all my sins. Many years later, I created an animated film to illustrate this encounter in a way that might have meaning for those like me who seek forgiveness from their child and from Jesus. It can be viewed at preparearoom.com.

Honoring our unborn child and making a space in our lives to remember her and love her has been vital to the healing process my husband and I went through. We named our little one Melody Chaia (which means "life" in Hebrew and was my mother's Hebrew name) and gathered our children together for an informal memorial service that took place on a wonderful walk in a redwood forest. Of course we don't know for sure that she is a girl, but we are doing the best we can with limited information.

The Jewish Messiah

One of the greatest joys of having Jesus live in my heart is that I have learned how very Jewish it is to follow the Jewish Messiah prophesied in the ancient Hebrew Scriptures by the Jewish prophets of old. Everything about being a follower of Jesus turns out to be so Jewish! So much about the so-called New Testament is not new—it has its roots in the so-called Old Testament. Even the idea of a "new testament" is found in the weeping prophet Jeremiah (Jeremiah 31:31–34). All the writers of the New Testament with the exception of Dr. Luke were Jewish. Jesus himself is recorded in the gospel accounts as having observed the Shabbat, Chanukah, Passover, and the other feasts of Israel. He is Jewish and brought salvation to the Jew first, and also to the Gentiles.

To my great delight and joy, I have not found it necessary to forsake my Jewish identity as a Christian—in fact, I'm more Jewish now than I ever was before. I am a Jewish follower of the Jewish Messiah. Becoming a Christian has given me an insatiable hunger to study my own Hebrew Scriptures and the Hebrew language and make the amazing connections between those writings and the New Testament writings. Most importantly, like all followers of Jesus, I am a sinner saved by grace. Because he took my sins on the cross, I have hope of eternal life.

Honoring the pattern of Romans 1:16 (to the Jew first), I crave to see my Jewish brothers and sisters embraced into the salvation of their Mashiach (Messiah, or Christ) Yeshua (Jesus), whose name means "God saves." My prayer is that the call of the Shema—the central prayer of Jewish faith found at Deuteronomy 6:4—will open their ears to hear the truth about who he is and the salvation he offers. He is for us. He is for you. I only know that if God has been faithful to keep my people in his plan of redemption throughout the millennia, his arm (his *zeroa*) is not too short to reach you.

I also crave to see my Jewish brothers and sisters in Israel who suffer from the hurt of abortion find the peace and healing that can only come from Yeshua. While all are welcome to this healing process, and while I rejoice to see any healed, this book was written specifically with these dear men and women in mind.

Shema, Yisrael, Adonai Eloheinu, Adonai echad.
Hear, O Israel: the Lord is our God, the Lord is one.

The Mourner's Kaddish[1]

Magnified and sanctified be God's great Name throughout the world which He has created according to His will.

May He establish His kingdom in your lifetime and during your days, and within the life of the entire House of Israel, speedily and soon; and say, Amen.

May His great name be blessed forever and to all eternity.

Blessed and praised, glorified and exalted, extolled and honored, adored and lauded be the name of the Holy One, blessed be He, beyond all the blessings and hymns, praises and consolations that are ever spoken in the world; and say, Amen.

May there be abundant peace from heaven, and life, for us and for all Israel; and say, Amen.

He who creates peace in His celestial heights, may He create peace for us and for all Israel; and say, Amen.

---

1. The Mourner's Kaddish is a prayer traditionally recited by Jews in honor of their departed loved ones.

Acknowledgments

Thank You, God, for using this Jonah. Please soften the hearts of the Ninevites for me! The rooms we prepare are Yours, the house is Yours, and unless You build the house, they labor in vain who build it. Like Jonah, I rejoice in declaring, "You have brought up my life from the pit.... Salvation is from the Lord!"

This book began with Robin Strom, director of the Marin Pregnancy Clinic, who sends troubled women my way. Thank you, Robin, for always making me smile. I treasure your warmth, courage, and faith in God and God in me. Gail Nordskog gave me motivation when she invited me to be part of her project *Hearts of Purpose*. I have sought to be worthy of that honor with this book. Thank you, Gail. Jerry Nordskog is my hero, a man of character who has blessed me beyond measure. Thank you, Jerry and the whole NPI team. I am so grateful to you, Ron Kirk, for guiding me with your keen inner compass to a truer message.

A number of "midwives" encouraged the book's birthing: Pastor Marcus and Melanie Small and People's Inter-Cities Fellowship, Myles and Katharine Weiss and Beth Shalom, Lesia Knudsen, Katie Philpott, Molly Landin, Karen Hoerdel, Marci Garl, Rae-chel Titus, Sarah Shelfer, and Nanette Jordan. A special thanks goes out to Kathi Shaw and Cheryl Geyer, my two dear friends whose friendship over tea has spanned a decade and borne much fruit. Cheryl, you shared Hannah Hurnard and gifted me with your skills and love. You live out Jesus's words, "Freely give"

(Matthew 10:8b). Kathi, you reminded me to let this book be my prayer for the peace of Jerusalem (Psalm 122:6). To Desta Garrett I owe an immeasurable debt of gratitude. You once told me I had a book in me, and you gave me the means to bring it forth. These and many others have my love and thanks.

Special thanks go out to the guest contributors, who stepped out of their comfort zones to talk about difficult stuff. Thank you all. Gaylord Enns and his book *Love Revolution*[1] continue to impact my understanding of the role of love in the healing process.

I particularly thank my husband Jerry, who truly deserves a co-writer credit. Jerry, your musical ear for language, your ability to see the big picture, and your ruthless honesty have been invaluable. This would have been half a book without you, as I am half a person without you.

I am inspired by the many women who have overcome their abortion experiences to thrive and bring hope to others—I'm thinking particularly of Peggy Sterling and Rose Romant Todd.

I am deeply indebted to those who pray for the confused and hurting women walking into abortion clinics every day. I was one of those, and someone prayed for me.

---

1. Gaylord Enns, *Love Revolution: Rediscovering the Lost Command of Jesus* (Chico, CA: Love Revolution Press, 2011).

About Prepare a Room Ministries

The book you hold in your hand is the centerpiece of Prepare a Room (**PAR**) Ministries. The purchase of this book supports **PAR**, which is dedicated to furthering the Gospel of Jesus Christ, with a focus on offering the healing work of the cross to those hurt by abortion.

We offer a variety of ways to support our efforts. Firstly, we invite you to **PAR**tner with us by donating to our ministry. You can donate through Patreon (patreon.com/preparearoom). **PAR**tners will receive periodic updates on our activities, and all donations are tax deductible. Or, consider purchasing one of our products as a way of supporting **PAR**:

Prepare a Room, the book

To order more copies of this book, visit NordskogPublishing.com or call them at 805-642-2070. *Quantity pricing available.*

Prepare a Cup Tea Blend

Yes, there really is a tea blend, crafted with you in mind! Loose herbal tea made from these fine ingredients: nettle, spearmint, lavender, lemon grass, licorice, rose. *Share a cup with a friend!*

Prepare a Room, the CD

"Prepare a Room," a collection of songs for those hurt by abortion, composed and performed by the author and her husband. Find the collection on iTunes and Spotify.

Find these products and learn more about us at PrepareARoom.com

Foundlings

Foundlings, Wee Ambassadors of God's Grace

If you have visited PrepareARoom.com, you have seen in full-color the **Foundlings** that you read about in the Epilogue of this book, and you know that they are numerous and their numbers are growing day by day. These original works of art are the author's commitment to giving a face to the faceless babies lost in abortion. These drawings can be yours today.

One way you can support Prepare a Room Ministries is to purchase a signed, full-color, 4 x 6-inch giclée print on archival artist paper of one of twelve **Foundlings** that have been selected for quantity production. Or you can purchase *any* **Foundling** of your choice for an additional cost.

Your own personal signed **Foundling** print is suitable for framing, or you can enjoy it privately within the acid-free presentation folder in which you will receive it.

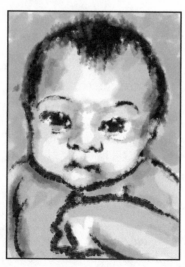

Contact us at PrepareARoom.com • michelle@PrepareARoom.com
Support us at patreon.com/preparearoom • 707-861-9408

HEARTS OF PURPOSE: *Real-life stories about ten ordinary women doing extraordinary things for the Glory of God*

THE GAIL GRACE NORDSKOG COLLECTION

In this age of suffering and great need, Gail Grace Nordskog highlights quiet and often unsung women heroes of modern-day society who have reached out to help. Their stories represent the true salt and light of the earth. Mrs. Nordskog invites her readers to seek God's will, and to live out their lives with action and a passion for God and others, using the gifts God alone gives as He wills.

We eagerly anticipate the follow-up volume of *Hearts of Purpose*, Volume 2, "The Battle," which is currently in production.

"My deepest desire is to encourage you to step out of your comfort zone, as these ten did, and live your life in fulfillment of your God-ordained purpose. May you be inspired to discover what that purpose is, and live it!"

— Gail Grace Nordskog

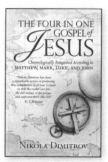